I0140778

RESTRICTED
FILE: FO

P-47 THUNDERBOLT
PILOT'S FLIGHT OPERATING INSTRUCTIONS

This manual is sold for historic research purposes only, as an entertainment.
It is not intended to be used as part of an actual flight training program. No
book can substitute for flight training by an authorized instructor. The licensing
of pilots is overseen by organizations and authorities such as the FAA and CAA.
Operating an aircraft without the proper license is a federal crime.

©2007-2010 Periscope Film LLC
All Rights Reserved
ISBN #978-1-935327-95-0   1-935327-95-X
www.PeriscopeFilm.com

The A. L. Garber Co., Ashland, O.—2-43, 20,000

JANUARY 20, 1943

*PILOT'S FLIGHT OPERATING
INSTRUCTIONS*

.

P-47B,-C,-D and -G
AIRPLANES

NOTE: This Technical Order replaces T. O. No. 01-65BC-1 dated Sept. 20, 1942 and T. O. No. 01-65BG-1, dated April 10, 1942.

NOTICE: This document contains information affecting the National Defense of the United States within the meaning of the Espionage Act, 50 U. S. C., 31 and 32, as amended. Its transmission or the revelation of its contents in any manner to an unauthorized person is prohibited by law.

PUBLISHED BY AUTHORITY OF THE COMMANDING GENERAL,
ARMY AIR FORCES, BY THE HEADQUARTERS,
AIR SERVICE COMMAND, PATTERSON FIELD, FAIRFIELD, OHIO

The A. L. Garber Co., Ashland, O.—2-43, 20,000

JANUARY 20, 1943

P-47B

Figure 1—Three-Quarter
Rear View of P-47B
Airplane

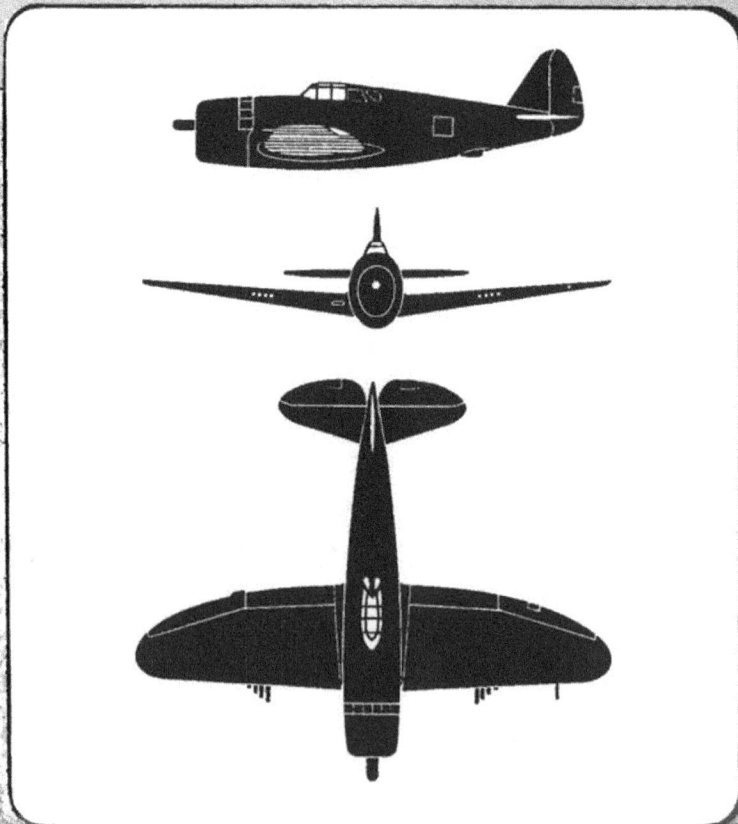

Figure 2—Three-Quarter Rear View of the P-47C, P-47D and P-47G Airplane

TABLE OF CONTENTS

APPENDIX

SECTION I
DESCRIPTION

1. AIRPLANE.

a. GENERAL.—The models P-47B, P-47C, P-47D, and P-47G are low-wing, singleplace, all metal monoplanes, each powered with a 2000-horsepower Pratt & Whitney radial engine. The P-47B, P-47C, and P-47D airplanes are manufactured by the Republic Aviation Corporation at Farmingdale, Long Island, New York, and at Evansville, Indiana. The P-47G airplanes are manufactured by the Curtiss-Wright Corporation at Buffalo, New York. The engine drives a four-bladed propeller. Hydraulically operated landing gear, wing flaps, tail wheel, and brakes are provided. The approximate over-all dimensions are as follows:

Length—P-47B: 34 feet, 10 inches; P-47C, -D, -G: 35 feet, 7 inches; Height—12 feet, 8 inches; Span—40 feet, 9⅝₆ inches.

b. ACCESS TO AIRPLANE.—A step and handholds are provided on the fuselage on the left side of the airplane. The canopy is unlatched by pressure on a small lever on the forward edge of the canopy, allowing it to slide back. Several locking positions are provided.

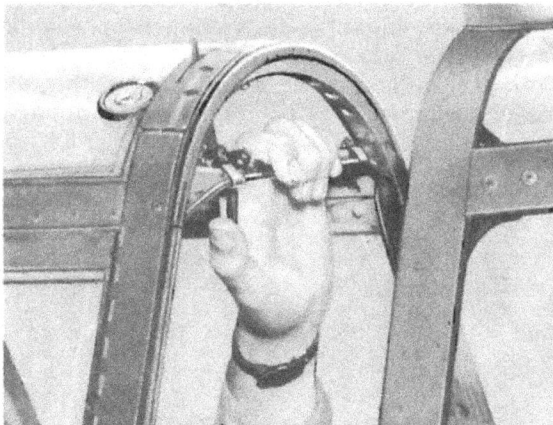

Figure 3—Canopy Latch Release

c. FUEL AND OIL.

(1) Fuel: Specification No. AN-VV-F-781, Amendment No. 5. Octane: grade 100.

NOTE

If Amendment No. 4 is used, take-off and military power manifold pressure *must be reduced 10 percent.*

(2) Oil: Specification No. AN-VV-O-446. Viscosity: grade 1120. (For cold-weather operation, use grade 1100 with oil dilution, if necessary.)

d. PILOT PROTECTION.

(1) ARMOR.—Front and rear armor protection sufficient to withstand U. S. .30, German, .312, and Japanese and Italian .303 (7.7mm)-caliber fire by direct right angle hit is provided for the pilot. Enemy fire originating within the areas graphically illustrated in figure 4 will not reach the pilot.

NOTE: AIRPLANE ARMOR PROTECTS PILOT FROM FIRE ORIGINATING WITHIN RED AREA.

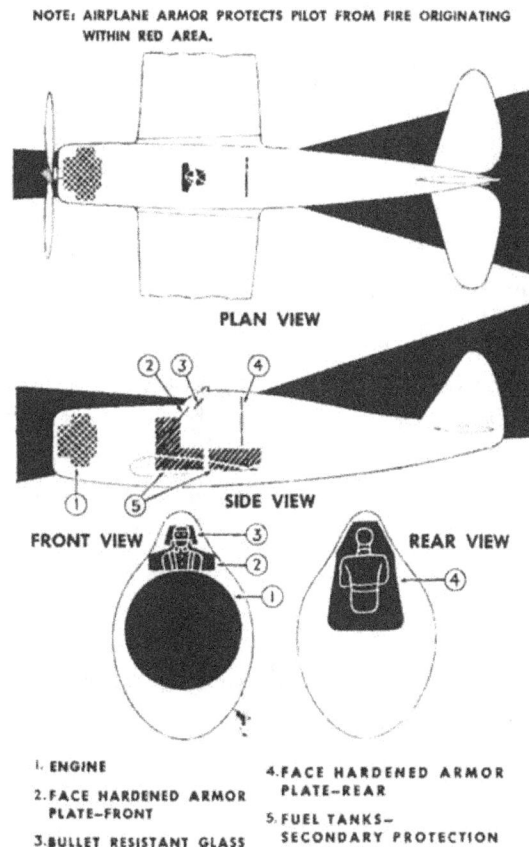

PLAN VIEW

SIDE VIEW

FRONT VIEW   REAR VIEW

1. ENGINE
2. FACE HARDENED ARMOR PLATE—FRONT
3. BULLET RESISTANT GLASS
4. FACE HARDENED ARMOR PLATE—REAR
5. FUEL TANKS—SECONDARY PROTECTION

Figure 4—Angles of Personnel Protection

(2) CRASH PROTECTION.—A crash protector is incorporated just aft of the pilot for turnover protection, and a welded crash skid is installed in the underside of the fuselage.

RESTRICTED

e. MOORING PROVISIONS.—Lugs for mooring the airplane are provided in the lower side of each wing ahead of Spar 1, just outboard of the landing gear leg and are usually concealed inside the wing. They are made available for use by pulling open the door marked "TIE-DOWN" and then pulling out the lugs. Lashing down the tail may be done by inserting a rope through either the lift tube or the tail wheel yoke.

2. POWER PLANT.

The Pratt & Whitney R-2800-21 engine is a twin-row, 18-cylinder, supercharged, air-cooled engine. There are both geared and turbine superchargers; the turbine-driven supercharger is a separate and remotely installed unit. A control on the throttle quadrant opens and closes the waste gates, permitting variation in speed of the turbine-driven unit.

3. PROPELLER.

The propeller is a four bladed Curtiss electrically controlled, constant speed, multi-position propeller.

KEEP YOUR EYES ON A WHIRLING PROPELLER

4. CONTROLS AND OPERATIONAL EQUIPMENT.

a. AIRPLANE CONTROLS.

(1) COCKPIT SEAT.—The seat may be adjusted for height by lifting the lock release handle on the right side of the seat (figure 5), and raising or lowering the seat as desired. To lock the seat in position, release the locking handle and "jiggle" the seat slightly in a vertical direction until its spring-loaded locking device definitely snaps into position. The seat is equipped with the standard shoulder harness with the spring-release or lock control on the left side.

(2) AILERON AND ELEVATOR.—Conventional.

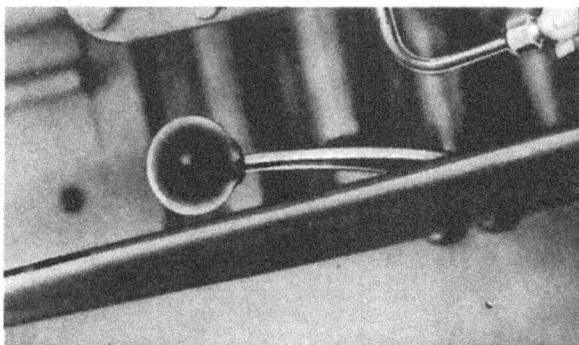

Figure 5—Seat Adjustment Lever

(3) FLIGHT CONTROLS LOCK.—The control stick and rudder pedals may be locked by means of a small red lever located at the base of the control stick. Push stick forward, reach down and pull red knob up and back so that the tongue aft of the red knob swings aft and down over a small hook on the forward side of the control stick. At the same time, the forward part of the knob assembly swings up and forward, pushing a long slender rod forward which clamps the two rudder pedals in position.

(4) RUDDER CONTROL.—Conventional pedals, hinged from the top, are equipped with conventional toe brakes. Each rudder pedal may be adjusted to desirable length by first pushing outboard on the spring-loaded adjustment lock (figure 7) which will permit the rudder pedal to float free on its hinge. After moving pedal to desired location, release the lock and "jiggle" the pedal slightly to allow the locking pin to snap into position. *Always adjust both pedals to the same length.*

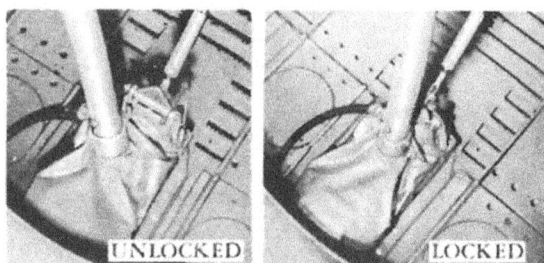

Figure 6—Flight Control Lock

(5) ELEVATOR TRIM TAB CONTROL.—Trim tabs may be adjusted in flight by a crank on the box on the left side of the cockpit. (See figure 9-3.) Rotate clockwise for nose down. Their extreme effectiveness renders this a source of danger, and care must be exercised to see that the trim tab wheel is rotated in the correct direction to produce the desired effect.

Figure 7—Rudder Pedal and Adjustment Lever

(6) RUDDER TRIM TAB CONTROL.—This tab may be adjusted in flight by turning the knob (figure 9-1) on the left side of the cockpit. Rotate knob clockwise for right rudder.

(7) AILERON TRIM TAB CONTROL.—The left aileron trim tab only is adjustable. It may be adjusted in flight by turning wheel (figure 9-4) clockwise for right wing down.

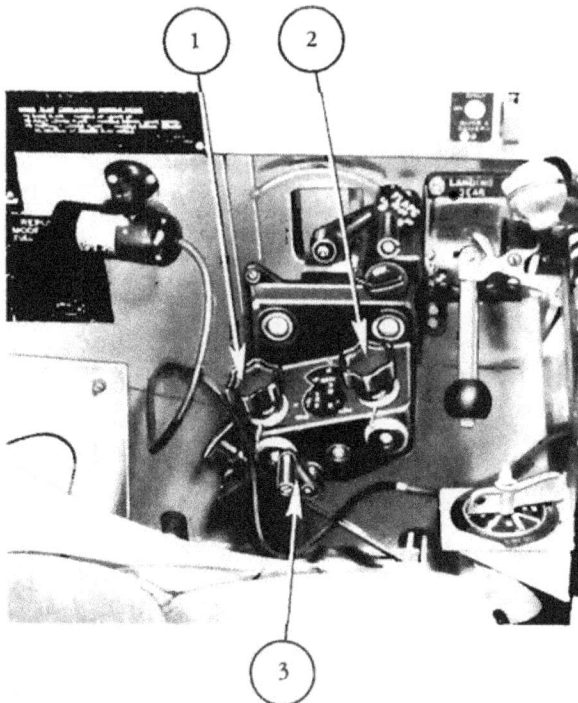

Figure 8—Trim Tab Controls—P-47C, P-47D, and P-47G

CAUTION

The aileron and rudder trim tab wheels on early airplanes do not work in the same plane as the controls they operate, and a danger exists that pilots may turn these controls in the wrong direction.

(8) LANDING GEAR CONTROL.

(a) The landing gear may be operated by means of either the engine-driven hydraulic pump or by the emergency hand pump.

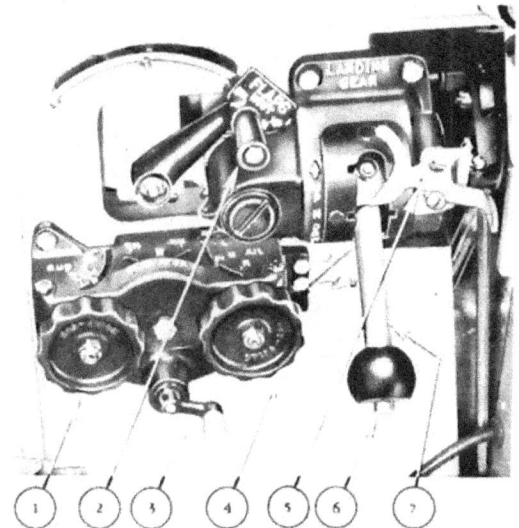

1. Rudder Tab Control
2. Flap Control
3. Elevator Tab Control
4. Aileron Tab Control
5. Landing Gear Safety Catch
6. Landing Gear Control Lever Button
7. Landing Gear Control Lever

Figure 9—Trim Tab, Landing Gear, and Wing Flap Controls, P-47B

(b) An indicator showing position of the wheels is mounted on the instrument panel. (See figure 30-1.) The usual warning horn indicates gear up when throttle is closed. The throttle arm controls a horn shut-off switch. If shut-off switch is thrown out, it will automatically be closed whenever the throttle is opened.

WARNING

On the P-47C, P-47D, and P-47G airplanes, the landing gear and wing flap indicator (figure 30-1), and the warning horn have been removed. A lamp on the instrument panel glows red when the gear is not locked down or is not completely retracted.

RESTRICTED

(9) WING FLAP CONTROL.—The wing flaps are actuated by engine hydraulic pressure with provision for emergency hand pump operation. They are actuated by means of the flap control switch (figure 9-2). The pressure on the flaps is equalized by means of the hydraulic equalizer valve located on the floor to the right of the pilot's seat (see figure 10). This valve insures that the two flaps come down or go up together.

Figure 10—Hydraulic Equalizer Valve

(10) TAIL WHEEL LOCK.—The retractable tail wheel may be interconnected with the rudder for control in taxying by means of a lever on the floor at the right of the pilot's seat. When the lever (figure 11) is placed in the forward position, the tail wheel is locked and disconnected from the rudder pedals. When the tail wheel is lowered after flight, it automatically falls into the locked position. P-47C-1RE and subsequent models have provisions for locking and free swiveling only and are not steerable.

Figure 11—Tail Wheel Lock

(11) HEATING AND VENTILATING CONTROLS.—Fresh air is controlled by a push-pull control (figure 12) on the right side of the cockpit. Adequate heat is supplied by the hot air type defroster which has a control (figure 13) mounted on the right side of the cockpit just behind the windshield.

Figure 13—Defroster Control

Figure 12—Cockpit Ventilator Control

(12) FUEL SYSTEM. (See figures 24 and 25.)

(a) TANKS.

1. There are two self-sealing tanks installed in the fuselage under and forward of the floor of the pilot's compartment. The main tank has a capacity of 205 U. S. gallons (171 Imp. gallons). The auxiliary tank has a capacity of 100 U. S. gallons (83 Imp. gallons), making a total capacity of 305 U. S. gallons (254 Imp. gallons).

2. There is a fuel level warning lamp for the main tank. It will come on when approximately 40 U. S. gallons (33 Imp. gal.) remain in the tank. The amount remaining for reserve will vary between 2 and 20 gallons, depending upon the altitude of the airplane during run out. When operating at low power and speed with a relatively high angle of attack, most of the fuel will be used up while on "MAIN," and when operating in a nose-low or high-speed condition, the main tank supply will be exhausted early, leaving a relatively large amount of fuel available on reserve. Because of the above defect, ten gallons (U. S.) should be kept in the auxiliary tank for a safe, known reserve.

Figure 14—Belly Tank Release—P-47C, P-47D, and P-47G

(b) BELLY TANK—P-47C, P-47D, AND P-47G.—A 200 U. S. gallon (166 Imp. gallon) external tank can be installed on the P-47C, P-47D, and P-47G airplanes underneath the fuselage fastened to a release mechanism built into the crash skid. After fuel has been exhausted from the external tank, the tank may be released by pushing the lock on the release handle (figure 14) aft and pulling up on the release handle.

(c) FUEL GAGE. — An electrically operated compound gage (figure 30-14) is provided. It reads correctly only when the airplane is in flying position. A three-point correction card is posted near the gage (figure 15) for determining the quantity of fuel aboard when the ship is on the ground. Due to the inherent design, the main fuel gage is not accurate below about 20 gallons.

Figure 15—Fuel Correction Card, P-47B

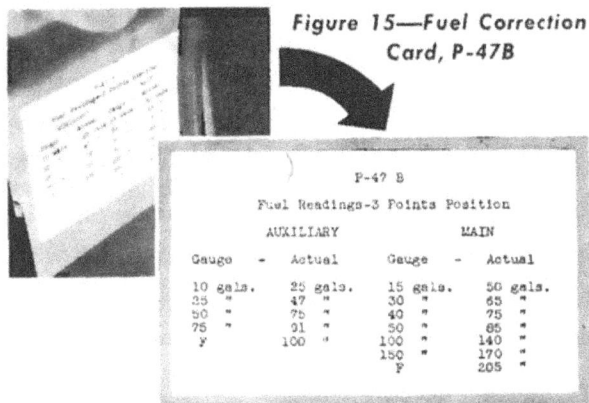

P-47 B

Fuel Readings-3 Points Position

	AUXILIARY		MAIN	
Gauge	-	Actual	Gauge	-	Actual
10 gals.		25 gals.	15 gals.		50 gals.
25 "		47 "	30 "		65 "
50 "		75 "	40 "		75 "
75 "		91 "	50 "		85 "
F		100 "	100 "		140 "
			150 "		170 "
			F		205 "

(d) FUEL SELECTOR VALVE.

1. The selector valve is conventional. When turning valve be sure to feel that the valve seats itself in the new position.

2. To operate on belly tank, control switch (figure 35-22) must be in the "ON" position, and the fuel selector valve (figure 16) must be in the "OFF" position. The external tank system is automatically turned off when the fuel selector cock is turned to any position other than "OFF" regardless of the position of the belly tank fuel control switch. (See figure 35-22.)

(e) FUEL PUMPS.

1. Fuel is supplied by means of a pump mounted directly on the engine, assisted by an electrically operated, variable-speed booster pump on the sump of each fuel tank. The booster pumps are turned on automatically by means of a rotary switch mounted on the fuel valve control shaft, when the fuel valve is

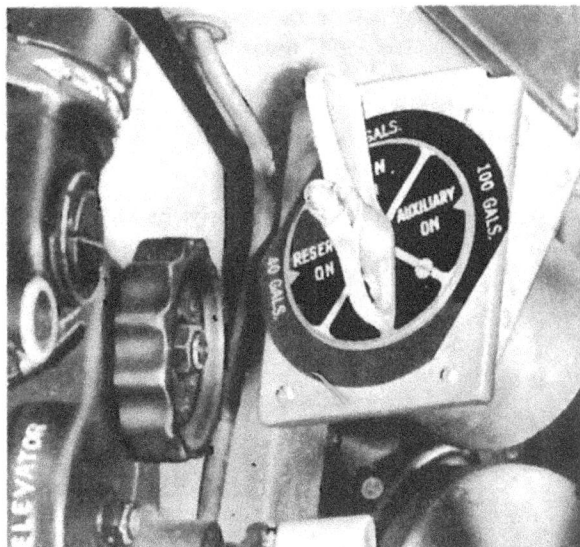

Figure 16—Fuel Selector Valve

turned to the "MAIN" and "AUXILIARY" positions respectively. Both pumps are turned off automatically when the fuel valve is turned to the "RESERVE" or "OFF" positions.

2. When either booster pump is turned on by placing the fuel cock in the "MAIN" or "AUXILIARY" position, the speed of that pump is controlled by the booster pump emergency rheostat which is located on the switch panel. (See figure 18-8.) This control has no "OFF" position. When turned to the extreme counter-clockwise position, marked "START AND ALTITUDE," the pump operates at its normal speed. Turning the knob clockwise increases the pump speed and therefore, the delivery pressure. Minimum pressure is 16 pounds per square inch; maximum is 17 pounds per square inch; idling is 7 pounds per square inch.

(13) OIL SYSTEM. *(See figure 26.)*

(a) TANK.—The oil tank is located in the upper part of the engine compartment with a filler on the left end of the tank and is accessible through the cowl door marked "OIL." The total capacity of the tank is 28 U. S. gallons (23 Imperial gallons), of which 19 U. S. gallons (16 Imperial gallons) is normal and the rest overload. The normal capacity is obtained by filling the tank until oil drips from the normal level pet cock (figure 26-3) on the left end of the tank below the filler.

(b) OIL COOLERS.—Two oil coolers are installed, one on each side in the lower part of the en-

gine compartment. Adjustable split doors are located in the exit ducts and are electrically operated and controlled from the cockpit by a switch (figure 18-11) on the main switch box. Shutter position indicators are located on the left side of the cockpit above the wing flap control handle (figure 17).

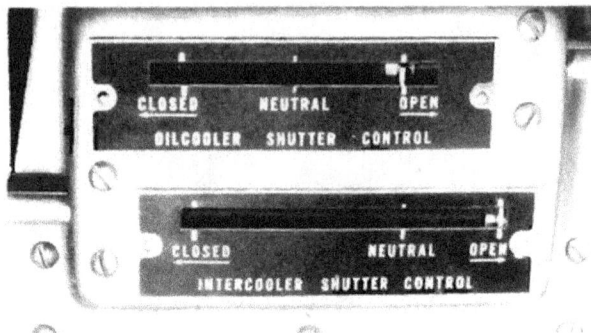

Figure 17—Oil Cooler and Intercooler Shutter Indicators

(c) INTERCOOLERS.—The heat of compression due to the turbine supercharger is removed from the inlet carburetor air by an intercooler. The intercooler exit is provided with sliding shutters, which are controlled by an electric switch on the main switch panel (figure 18-10).

(d) OIL PRESSURES.

Maximum: 90 pounds per square inch.
Minimum: 60 pounds per square inch.
Idling: 25 pounds per square inch.
Desired: 75-85 pounds per square inch.

(e) OIL DILUTION.—Provisions are made for oil dilution for cold-weather starting or for emergency operation. The oil dilution switch (figure 18-15) is located on the main switch panel.

(14) COWL FLAPS.—A control handle (figure 40) on the small panel at the right end of the instrument panel operates the cowl flaps. Pull it to open flaps and push to close. Intermediate settings can be obtained by releasing the knob when the desired opening has been reached. The knob will automatically return to neutral and the cowl flaps will remain in the intermediate position.

(15) LIGHTS.

(a) COCKPIT LIGHTS.—The ignition switch (figure 30-13) must be turned to "BAT" before any lights will function.

NOTE

On P-47C, P-47D, and P-47G airplanes, the master battery switch (figure 31-18) must be turned "ON."

Two fluorescent lights (figure 30-2), one on each side of the cockpit, and a light above the switch box (figure 34-8) provide extra illumination. On the P-47G airplane, the fluorescent lights (figure 19-B) have been eliminated and fluorescent and white light is furnished by two spotlights, one on each side of the cockpit. Switches (figures 18-3 and 18-4) are located on the main switch box.

(b) LANDING LIGHT.—A landing light is provided in the left wing. After the switch (figure 18-5) has been turned "ON," the light will not glow until after the landing light mechanism has extended the lamp to its operating position. Do not operate the light at speeds in excess of 200 mph, or for a longer period than necessary.

(c) IDENTIFICATION LIGHTS. (P-47B AIRPLANE ONLY.)—The identification light switches (figure 20) are mounted on the aft end of a small box to the right of the pilot just above the radio controls. The box also has a keying button on top.

NOTE

The identification lights and switches (figure 20) have been eliminated on the P-47C, P-47D, and P-47G airplanes.

(16) CANOPY.—The sliding canopy is provided with kick-out panels which are released by moving the handles marked "EMERGENCY RELEASE." Spoilers for use at very high speeds are provided to aid the pilot in opening the canopy. The spoilers are operated by pulling the small wire ring on the right forward side of the canopy. Normal operation is by means of the latch at the top front (see figure 46).

(17) PARKING BRAKE.—To park, pull parking brake handle (figure 21) and depress the pedals. To release, depress the pedals.

b. ENGINE CONTROLS.

(1) THROTTLE.—Additional supercharging for this engine is furnished by an exhaust-driven turbine supercharger. The engine is controlled by the conventional throttle, propeller and mixture controls. The supercharger is controlled by a control located outboard of the throttle. On P-47C and subsequent models,

1. Automatic-Manual Propeller Control Switch "Increase-Decrease" rpm Manual Control Switch
2. Propeller Control Breaker Switch
3. Instrument Light Switch
4. Cockpit Light Switch
5. Landing Light Switch
6. Position Lights Control
7. Compartment Lights Control
8. Electric Fuel Pump Rheostat
9. Circuit Breakers
10. Intercooler Shutter Switch
11. Oil Cooler Shutter Switch
12. Gun Sight Light Rheostat
13. Generator Switch
14. Fuel Warning Light Test Switch
15. Oil Dilution Switch
16. Pilot Tube Heat Switch
17. Ammeter

Figure 18—Main Switch Box, P-47B

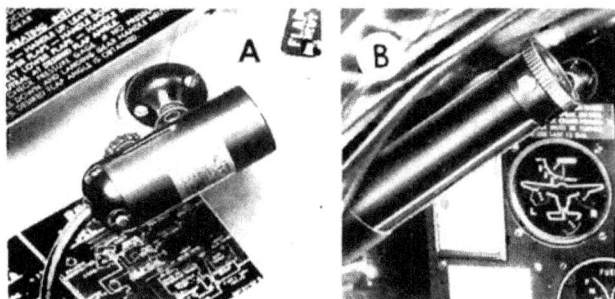

Figure 19—Spot and Fluorescent Lights

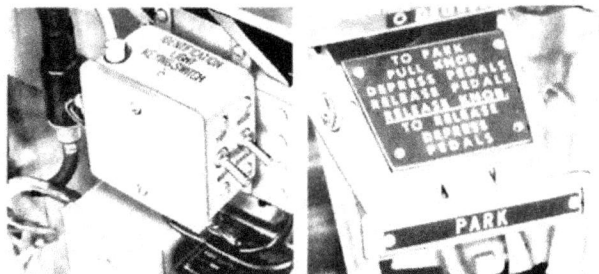

Figure 20—Identification Light Switches, P-47B

Figure 21—Parking Brake Control Handle

the throttle, supercharger control, and propeller control are so made that they can all be pushed forward by use of the throttle alone. When properly adjusted, this position should give about 52 inches Hg and 2700 rpm at altitudes up to 25,000 feet. It may be necessary to push past the stop to obtain full power above 25,000 feet. When the controls are connected, the supercharger control will come back as the throttle is retarded, but the propeller control will remain at the farthest advanced position. Rpm must be reduced by pulling the propeller control back.

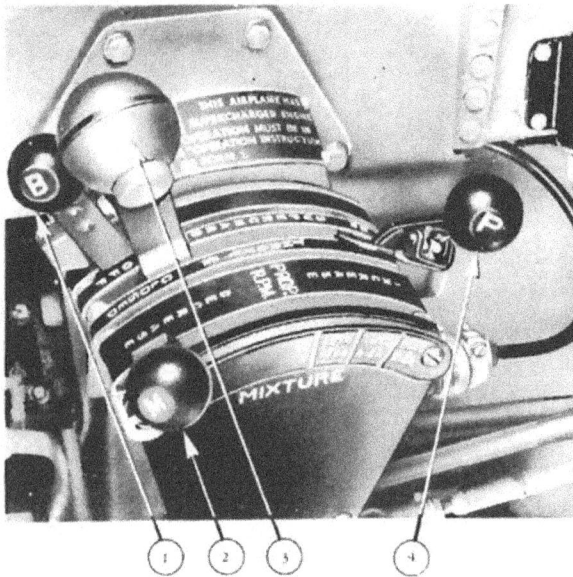

Figure 22—Throttle Quadrant

(2) MIXTURE CONTROL. — Four positions: "IDLE CUT-OFF," "AUTO-LEAN," "AUTO-RICH," and "FULL RICH."

(3) PROPELLER CONTROLS.

(a) "ON"-"OFF" switch (figure 18-2).

(b) Selector switch (figure 18-1) with positions for "AUTO," "INC RPM," and "DEC RPM."

(c) Governor lever (figure 22-4) on throttle quadrant.

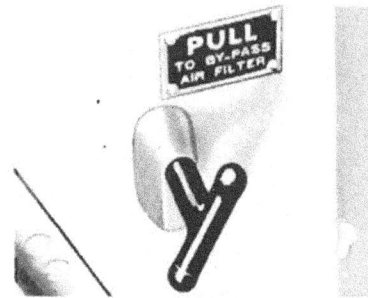

Figure 23—Air Filter Control

(4) AIR FILTER.—A push-pull control (figure 23) is provided on the left side of the rear wall of the cockpit to allow the bypassing of the air filter. Pull to bypass filter and push to attain full use of the filter. The use of this filter is recommended when atmospheric conditions so direct; i.e., dusty ground conditions or sand. The filter should be in the bypass position in clear air for maximum power plant efficiency. Use the bypass if there is a noticeable manifold pressure drop while using filter in icing conditions.

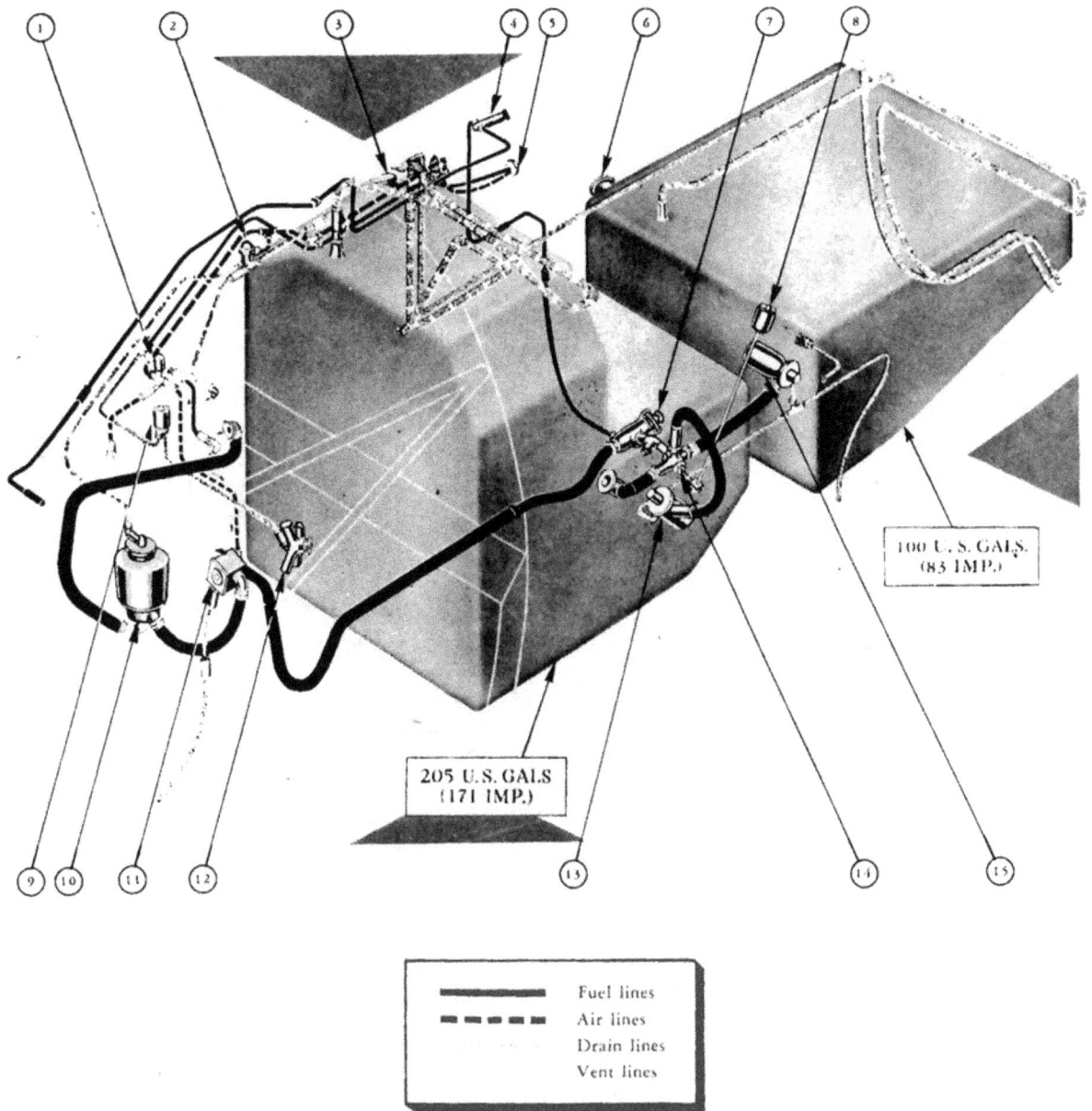

RESTRICTED

Legend:
- Fuel lines
- Air lines
- Drain lines
- Vent lines

100 U.S. GALS. (83 IMP.)

205 U.S. GALS (171 IMP.)

1. Pressure Warning System
2. Vapor Pressure Control Valve
3. Main Tank Filler Neck
4. Engine Primer
5. Pressure Gage
6. Auxiliary Tank Filler Neck
7. Strainer
8. Fuel Selector Valve Control Handle
9. Oil Dilution Solenoid
10. Vapor Eliminator
11. Engine-Driven Pump
12. "Y" Drain Cock
13. Main Booster Pump
14. Selector Valve
15. Auxiliary Booster Pump

Figure 24—Fuel System Diagram, P-47B

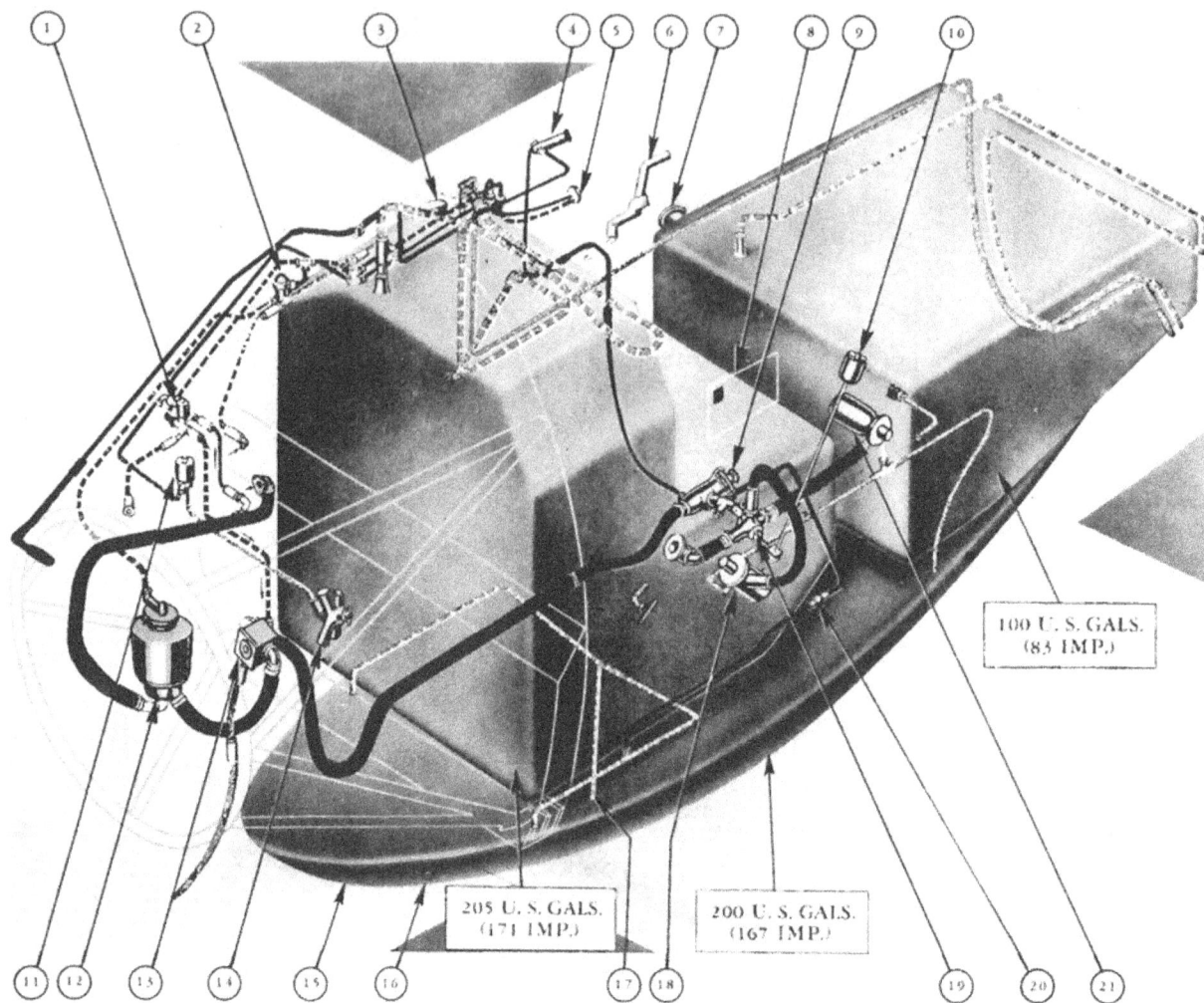

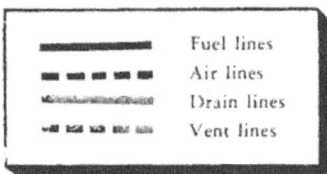

100 U. S. GALS.
(83 IMP.)

205 U. S. GALS.
(171 IMP.)

200 U. S. GALS.
(167 IMP.)

Fuel lines
Air lines
Drain lines
Vent lines

1. Pressure Warning System
2. Vapor Pressure Control Valve
3. Main Tank Filler Neck
4. Engine Primer
5. Pressure Gage
6. Belly Tank Release Handle
7. Auxiliary Tank Filler Neck
8. Belly Tank Control Switch
9. Strainer
10. Fuel Selector Valve Control Handle
11. Oil Dilution Solenoid
12. Vapor Eliminator
13. Engine-Driven Pump
14. "Y" Drain Cock
15. Belly Tank
16. Belly Tank Filler Neck
17. Belly Tank Vent
18. Main Booster Pump
19. Selector Valve
20. Solenoid Valve
21. Auxiliary Booster Pump

Figure 25—Fuel System Diagram, P-47C, P-47D, and P-47G

Drain lines
Vent lines
Oil lines

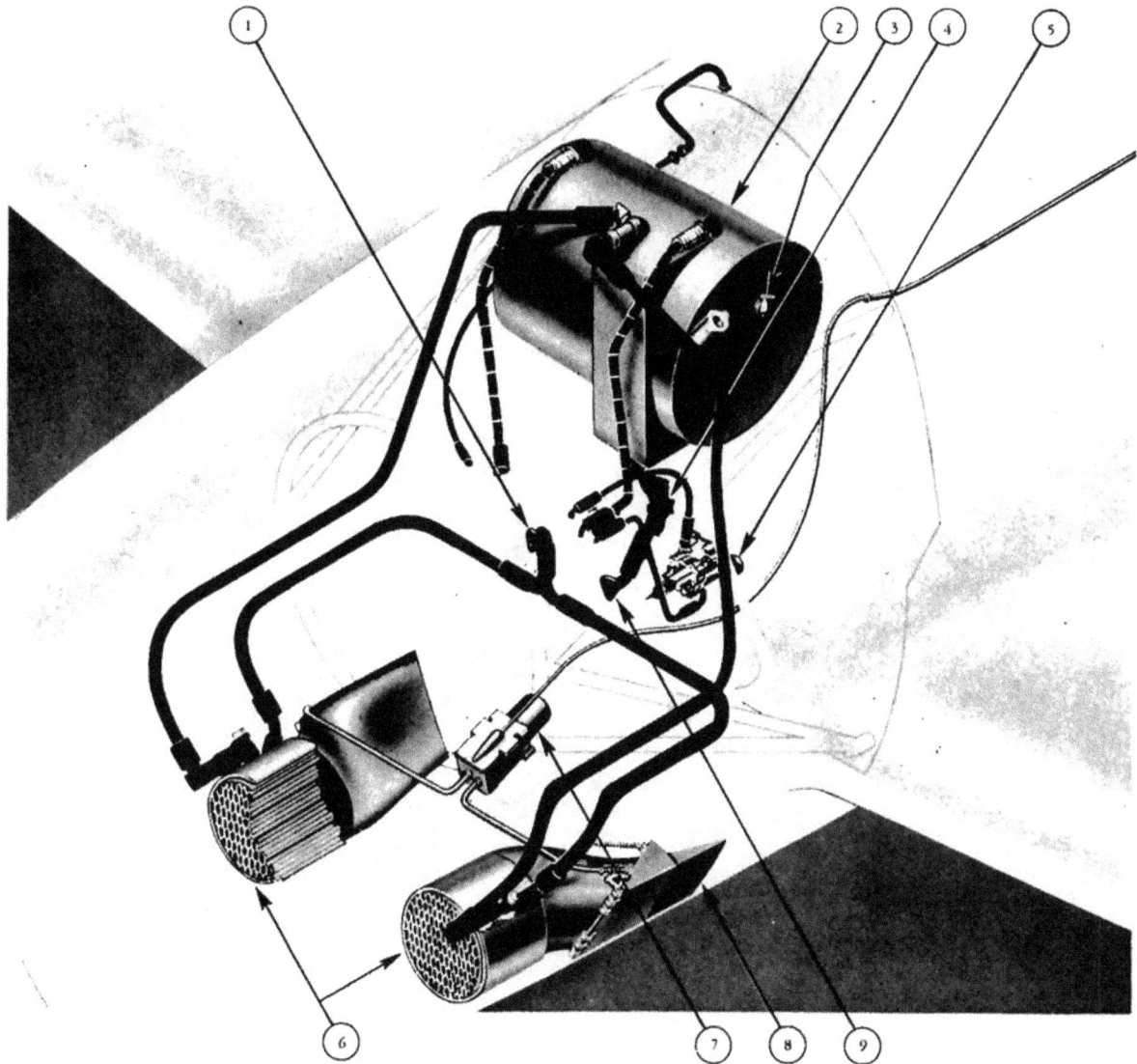

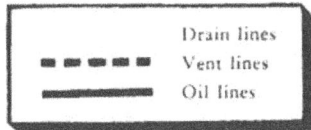

1. Oil from Engine
2. Hopper Type Tank
3. Oil Level Pet Cock
4. Connection for Oil Dilution
5. Supercharger Regulator
6. Oil Coolers
7. Temperature Regulator
8. Air Outlet Duct
9. Oil to Engine

Figure 26—Oil System Diagram

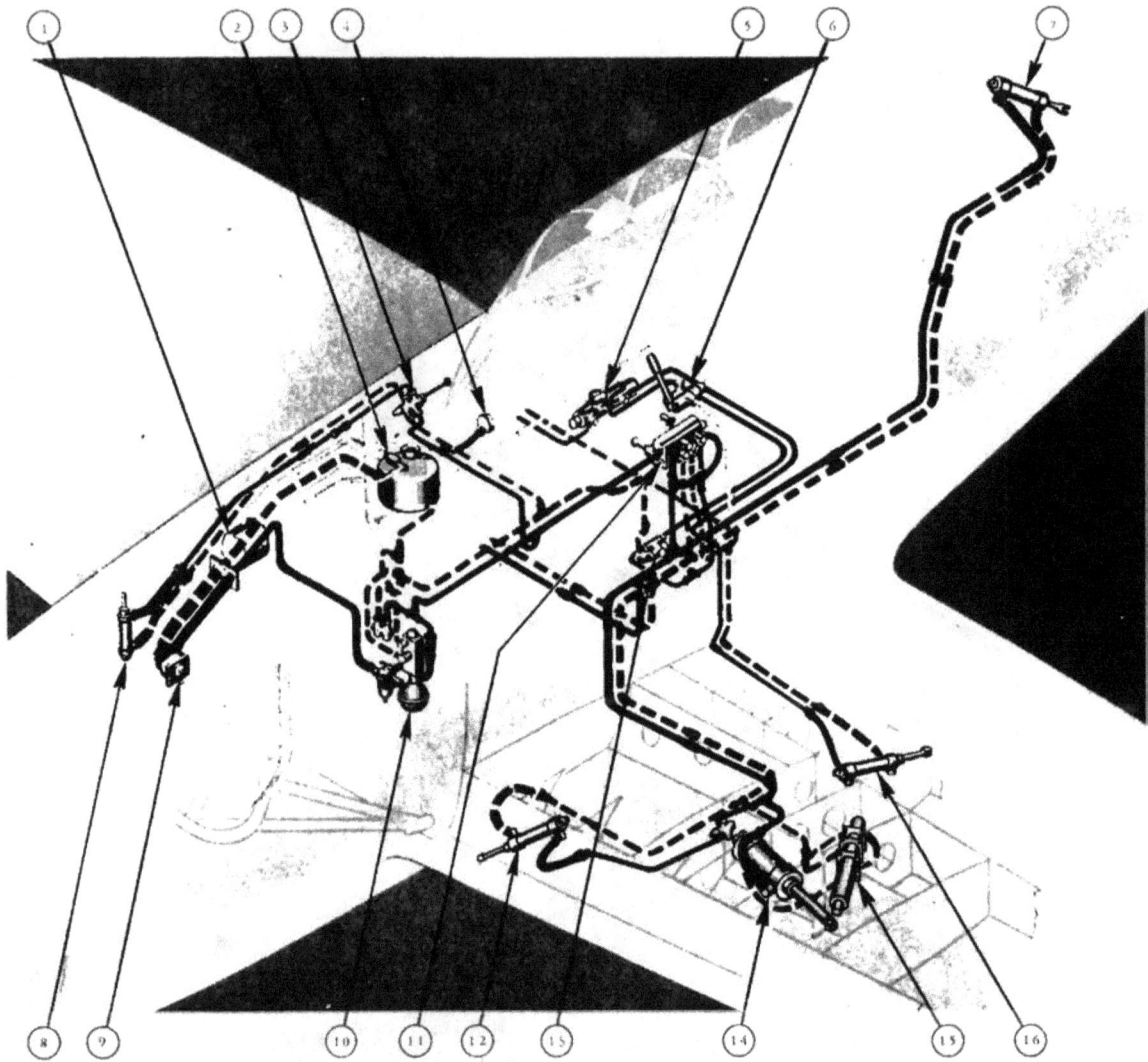

Figure 27—Hydraulic System Diagram

1. Carburetor Air Duct
2. Tank
3. Cowl Flap Valve
4. Pressure Gage
5. Equalizer Cylinder
6. Hand Pump

7. Tail Wheel Cylinder
8. Cowl Flap Cylinder
9. Engine-Driven Pump
10. Hydraulic Units
11. Selector Valve

12. Landing Gear Door Cylinder
13. Relief Valve
14. Landing Gear Cylinder
15. Downlock Cylinder
16. Flap Cylinder

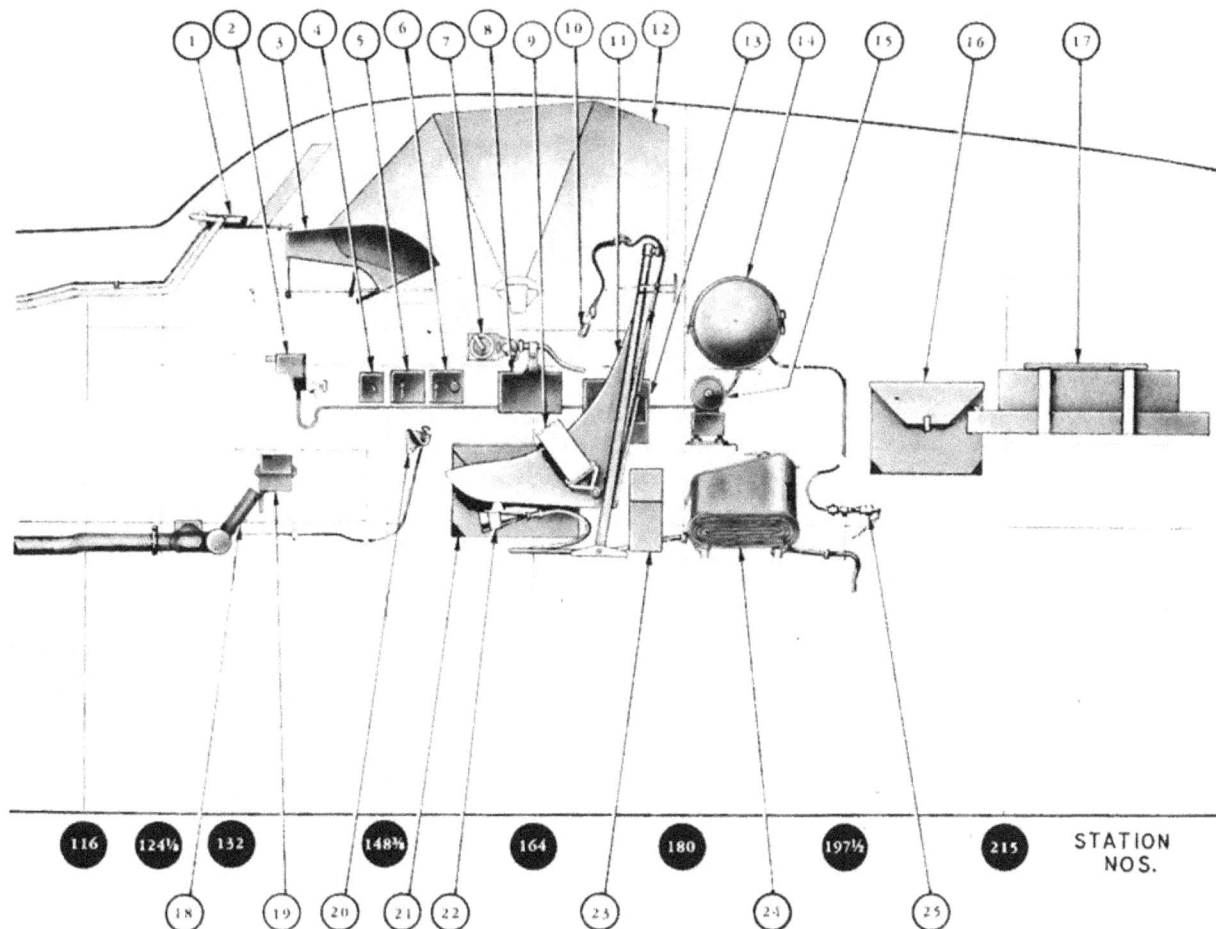

Figure 28—Balance Diagram and Fuselage Contents Arrangement—P-47B

1. Windshield Defroster
2. Oxygen Regulator
3. Anti-Glare Shield
4. Switch Box Radio
5. Control Box—Transmitter
6. Control Box—Receiver
7. Tuning Unit—Receiver
8. Check List Holder
9. Safety Belt
10. Shoulder Harness
11. Pilot Seat
12. Blind Flying Hood
13. First-Aid Kit

14. Oxygen Cylinder
15. Dynamotor
16. Data Case
17. Receiver and Transmitter Radio
18. Cockpit Ventilator
19. Radio Receiver Crystal Filter
20. Control—Cockpit Vent
21. Map Case
22. Pilot's Relief Tube
23. Pyotechnics
24. Engine Cover and Canopy Cover
25. Filler Valve—Oxygen

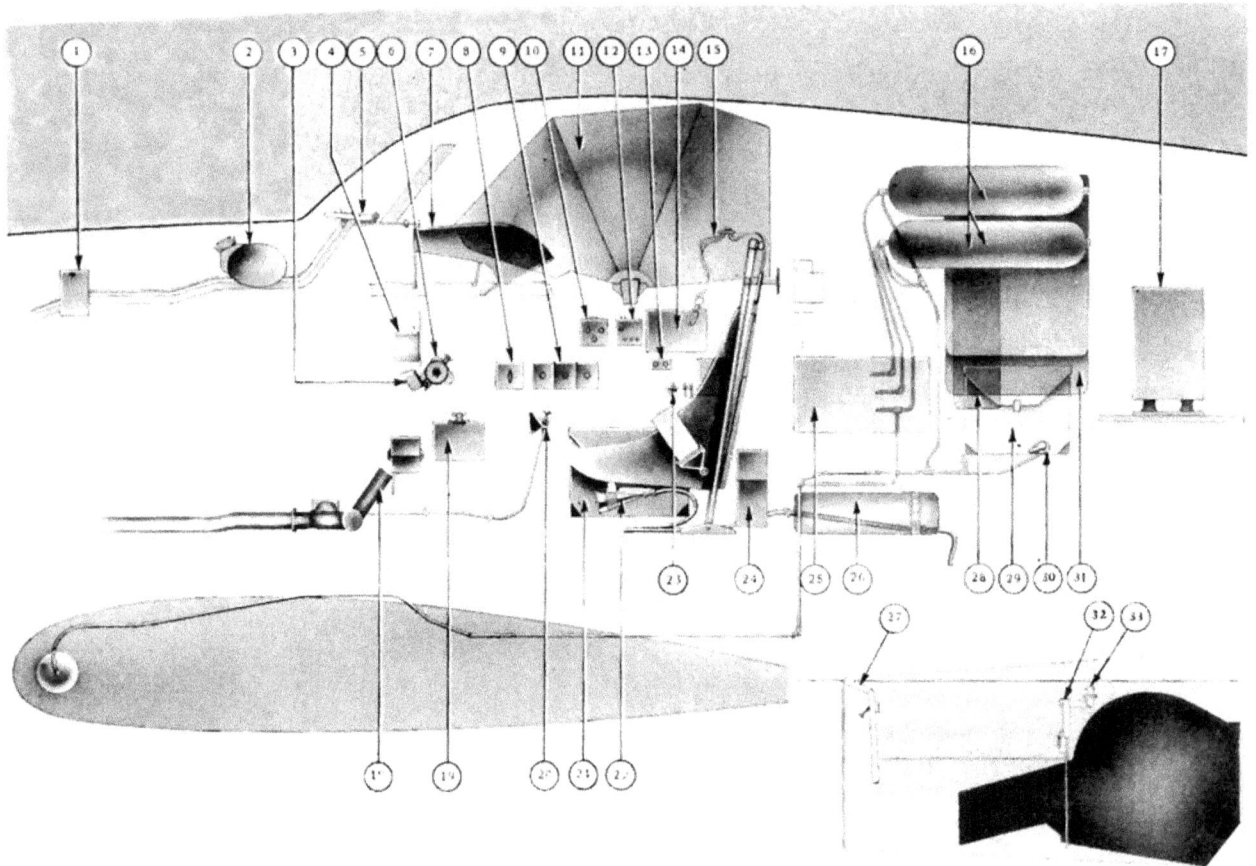

1. Dynamotor
2. Anti-Icing Equipment
3. Oxygen Pressure and Flow Indicator
4. Contactor (Pip Squeak)
5. Windshield Defroster
6. Oxygen Regulator
7. Anti-Glare Shield
8. Crystal Filter Selector Switch Box
9. Receiver Control Unit
10. Transmitter Control Box
11. Blind Flying Hood
12. Identification Lights Switch Box
13. IFF Detonator Switch Box
14. First-Aid Kit
15. Shoulder Harness
16. Oxygen Bottles
17. Radio Command Receiver
18. Cockpit Ventilator
19. Check List Holder
20. Cockpit Vent Control
21. Map Case
22. Relief Tube
23. Contactor Heater Switch Box
24. Pyotechnics
25. Radio Command Transmitter
26. Tool Kit
27. Ground Charging Tool
28. Mooring Kit
29. Data Case
30. Oxygen System Filler Valve
31. Engine and Canopy Cover
32. Starter Crank Extension
33. Starter Crank

Figure 29—Fuselage Contents Arrangement Diagram—P-47C, P-47D, and P-47G

1. Landing Gear, Tail Wheel and Flap Position Indicator
2. Fluorescent Light
3. Fuel Level Warning Lamp
4. Turn Indicator
5. Air-Speed Indicator
6. Bank and Turn Indicator
7. Artificial Horizon
8. Fuel Pressure Warning Light
9. Suction Gage
10. Vacuum Gage Selector Valve
11. Carburetor Air Temperature Gage
12. Propeller Anti-Icer Control
13. Ignition Switch
14. Fuel Quantity Gage
15. Kollsman Altimeter
16. Hydraulic Pressure Gage
17. Compass
18. Parking Brake
19. Clock
20. Rate of Climb Indicator
21. Tachometer
22. Manifold Pressure Gage
23. Fuel Pressure Gage
24. Oil Temperature and Pressure Gage
25. Cylinder Head Temperature Gage

Figure 30—Instrument Panel—P-47B

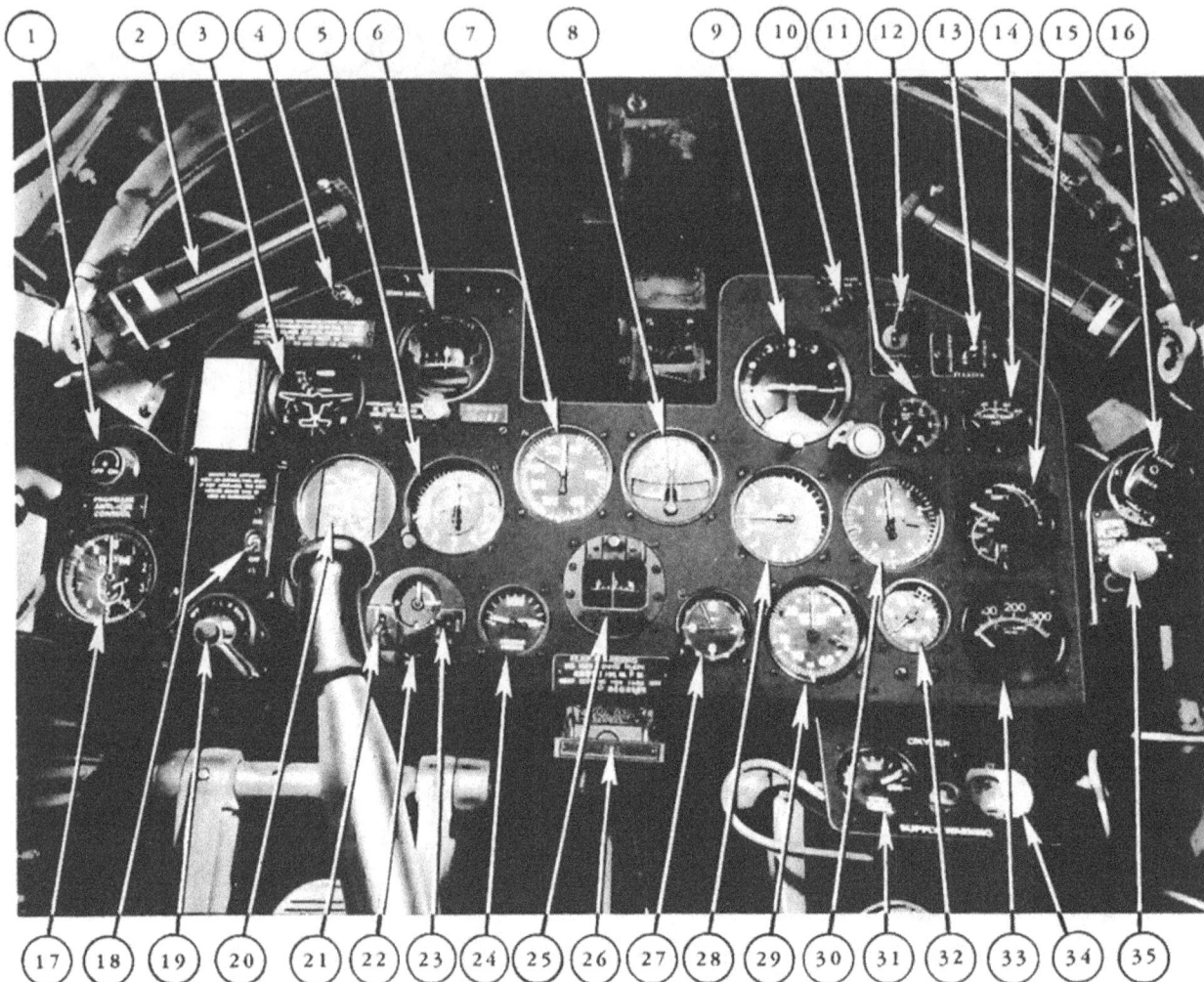

1. Propeller Anti-Icer Control
2. Fluorescent Light
3. Landing Gear Tail Wheel and Flap Position Indicator
4. Fuel Level
5. Altimeter
6. Turn Indicator
7. Air-Speed Indicator
8. Bank and Turn Indicator
9. Artificial Horizon
10. Fuel Pressure Warning Lamp
11. Suction Gage
12. Vacuum Gage Selector Valve
13. Starter Switch
14. Carburetor Air Temperature Gage
15. Oil Temperature and Pressure Gage
16. Engine Primer
17. Turbo Tachometer
18. Master Battery Switch
19. Ignition Switch
20. Fuel Quantity Gage
21. Contactor Switch
22. Contactor (Pip Squeak)
23. Contactor Clock Switch
24. Hydraulic Pressure Gage
25. Compass
26. Parking Brake Handle
27. Clock
28. Rate of Climb Indicator
29. Manifold Pressure Gage
30. Tachometer
31. Oxygen Cylinder Pressure Gage
32. Fuel Pressure Gage
33. Cylinder Head Temperature Gage
34. Oxygen Flow Indicator
35. Cowl Flap Control

Figure 31—Instrument Panel—P-47C, P-47D, and P-47G

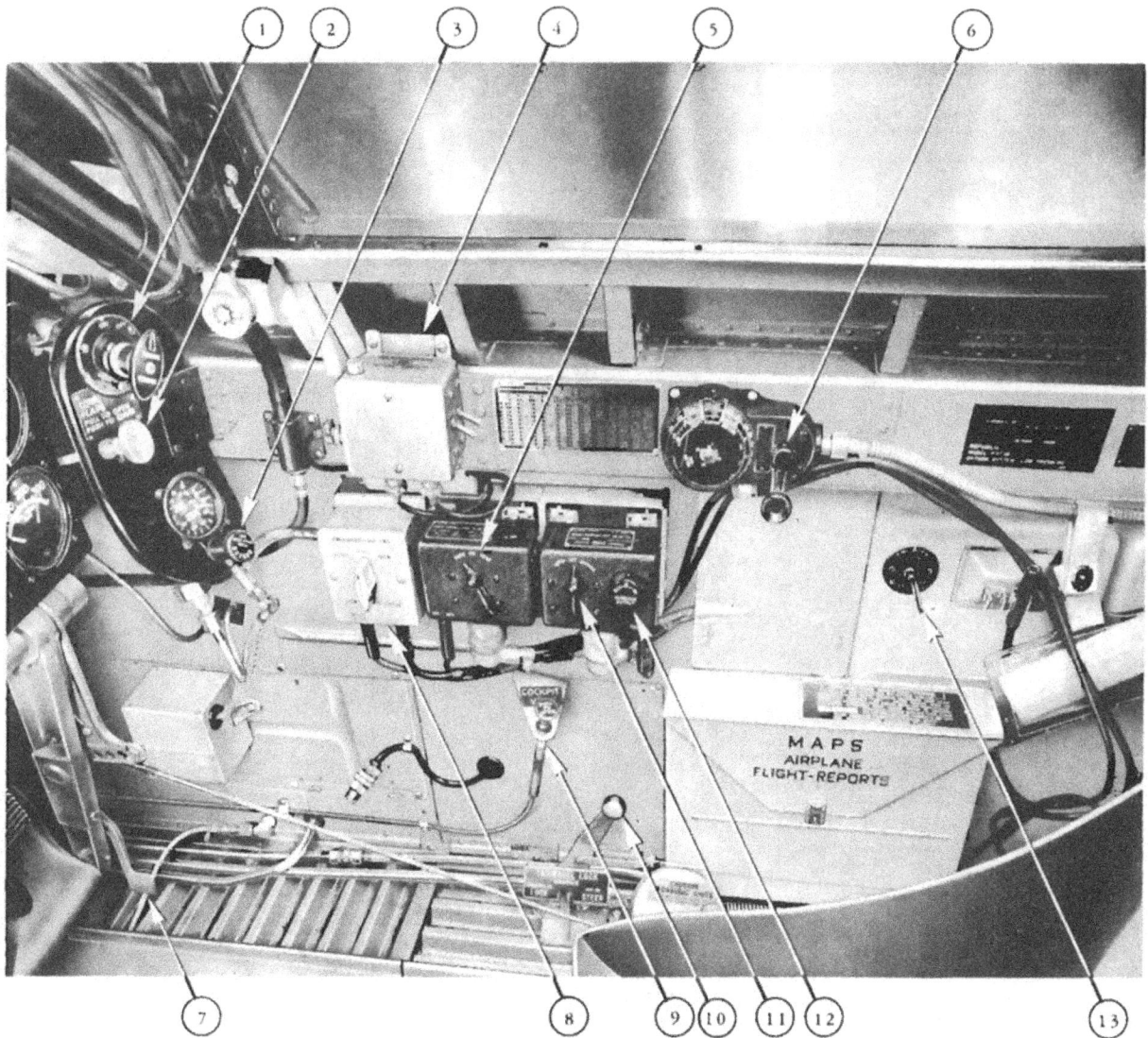

Figure 32—Cockpit—Right Side View—P-47B

1. Engine Primer
2. Cowl Flap Control
3. Oxygen Regulator
4. Identification Keying Switches
5. Transmitter Emission Control Switch
6. Radio Tuning Dial Control
7. Rudder Pedal Adjustment Lever
8. Radio Switch Box
9. Cockpit Vent Control
10. Tail Wheel Lock
11. Radio Receiver Volume Control Selector Switch
12. Radio Receiver and Transmitter Filament "Off-On" Control Knob
13. "Hi-Lo" Switch

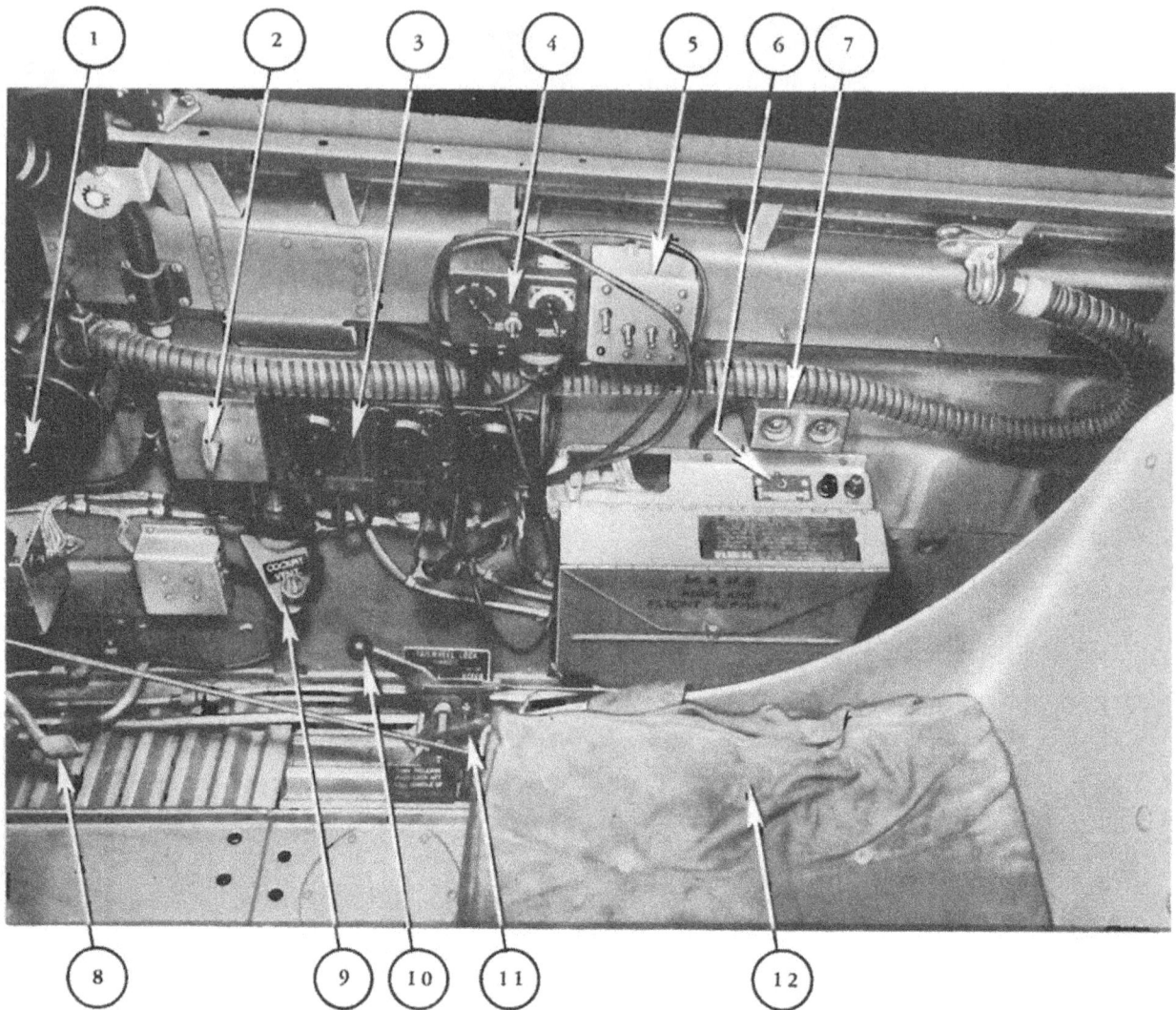

Figure 33—Cockpit—Right Side View—P-47C, P-47D, and P-47G

1. Oxygen Regulator
2. Crystal Filter Selector Switch
3. Command Receiver Control Box
4. Command Transmitter Control Box
5. Identification Lights Switches
6. Contactor Heater Switch
7. IFF Radio Destroyer Buttons
8. Rudder Pedal Adjustment Lever
9. Cockpit Vent Control
10. Tail Wheel Lock
11. Belly Tank Release
12. Pilot's Seat

1. Spotlight
2. Trim Tab Control Group
3. Flap Control Lever
4. Shutter Position Indicators
5. Gun Safety Switch
6. Propeller Safety Light
7. Throttle Quadrant
8. Panel Light

9. Landing Gear Warning Horn Switch
10. Propeller Anti-Icer Control
11. Ignition Switch
12. Gun Heat Control Lever
13. Safety Latch
14. Landing Gear Control Lever
15. Fuel Selector Valve
16. Main Switch Box
17. Circuit Breakers

Figure 34—Cockpit—Left Side View—P-47B

Figure 35—Cockpit—Left Side View, P-47C, P-47D, and P-47G

1. Cockpit Spotlight
2. Wing Flap Control Handle
3. Intercooler Shutter Indicator
4. Oil Cooler Shutter Indicator
5. Landing Gear Control Safety Latch
6. Gun Safety Switch
7. Throttle
8. Supercharger Control
9. Microphone Push-to-Talk Button
10. Mixture Control
11. Propeller Control
12. Landing Gear Warning Horn Switch
13. Propeller Anti-Icing Control
14. Rudder Trim Tab Control
15. Elevator Trim Tab Control Crank
16. Aileron Trim Tab Control
17. Landing Gear Control Handle
18. Fuel Selector Valve
19. Hydraulic Hand Pump
20. Main Switch Box
21. Circuit Breakers
22. Belly Tank Control Switch
23. Control Stick Grip

SECTION II
PILOT'S OPERATING INSTRUCTIONS

1. BEFORE ENTERING PILOT'S COMPARTMENT.

Ascertain that loading is in accordance with any of the alternate loading columns included on the appropriate Weight and Balance Chart in section III.

2. ON ENTERING THE PILOT'S COMPARTMENT.

a. SPECIAL CHECK FOR NIGHT FLYING.

(1) P-47B: Turn ignition switch to "BAT." P-47C, P-47D, and P-47G: Master battery switch "ON."

(2) Turn cockpit spotlights and fluorescent lights "ON."

(3) Test-operate gun sight light brilliancy.

(4) Test-operate position lights.

(5) Test-operate compartment lights.

(6) Test-operate landing light. Be sure that the light is retracted after test.

WARNING

Do not operate landing light for more than 5 seconds.

b. CHECK FOR ALL FLIGHTS.

(1) P-47B Airplane: Ignition switch "OFF." P-47C, P-47D, and P-47G: Ignition switch and master battery switch "OFF."

(2) Landing gear handle "DOWN."

(3) Flaps "UP." (Handle must be left in "UP" position.)

(4) Flap equalizer "CLOSED" (down).

(5) Generator switch "ON."

(6) P-47B: Ignition switch to "BAT." P-47C, P-47D, and P-47G: Ignition switch "OFF," and master battery switch "ON."

(7) Intercooler shutters "NEUTRAL."

(8) Oil cooler shutters "NEUTRAL."

(9) Propeller switch "ON." Selector in "AUTOMATIC."

(10) Fuel boost pump to "START AND ALTITUDE" (fully counterclockwise).

(11) Check fuel pressure.

(12) Gun switch "OFF."

3. STARTING ENGINE.

a. Turn propeller several revolutions by hand with ignition "OFF."

b. P-47B: Ignition switch "BAT."

c. P-47C, P-47D, and P-47G: Master battery switch "ON."

d. Supercharger lever "OFF" (full rear position).

e. Fuel selector valve "MAIN."

f. Crack throttle 1 inch to $1\frac{1}{2}$ inches open.

g. Mixture control "IDLE CUT-OFF."

h. Propeller switch "AUTOMATIC." Circuit breaker "ON."

i. Propeller control MAXIMUM RPM: 2700 rpm.

j. Fuel boost pump control on "START AND ALTITUDE."

k. Prime 2 to 4 strokes if hot, and 4 to 6 if cold. As much as one-fourth throttle opening and heavy priming may be necessary in extreme cold.

l. Ignition switch to "BOTH."

m. Energize at least 15 seconds and engage starter.

n. When engine starts, move mixture control to "AUTO-RICH" and throttle to 900 rpm.

CAUTION

Failure to keep mixture control in "IDLE CUT-OFF" position unless engine is running, will result in flooding and fire hazard.

o. Correct boost pump on tank is selected automatically by fuel selector valve.

4. ENGINE WARM-UP.

a. Check oil pressure at once. If not 25 pounds in 30 seconds, shut off engine.

b. Oil pressure will go to about 150 pounds to 200 pounds. DO NOT INCREASE power above 1000 rpm until pressure drops to normal.

c. Run at 800 rpm to 1000 rpm until pressure is normal and oil temperature is 40°C (104°F). In cold weather, close oil shutter and cowl flaps during warm-up. During warm weather, open cowl flaps and leave oil shutter at neutral. Avoid prolonged running on the ground and always keep cowl flaps open during long ground runs to prevent burning of ignition harness.

5. EMERGENCY TAKE-OFF.

Use oil dilution to obtain proper oil pressure at moderate power, and TAKE OFF!

WARNING

Apply throttle slowly but steadily. Too sudden application of throttle seriously affects torque.

6. ENGINE AND ACCESSORIES TEST.

a. When warm, and with propeller control set for maximum rpm, check magneto as follows:

(1) Turn propeller selector to "MANUAL."

(2) Open throttle to 2000 rpm, 30 inches Hg, and test each magneto. Drop in rpm should not exceed 50 on either magneto.

(3) Return propeller switch to "AUTOMATIC" and check full power at 45 inches Hg. Move supercharger control to "FULL ON" and check for 52 inches Hg. Full power check is not required for each flight. Tail must be tied down and wheels chocked to take propeller thrust when running engine above 2000 rpm.

CAUTION

When running at high power, NEVER CLOSE throttle with supercharger control "ON."

b. Check proper functioning of propeller by operating control.

c. Check for generator charge on ammeter.

d. With flap selector handle "UP" (fully forward), open flap equalizer valve (figure 10) on floor at right of seat for a minimum of 10 seconds and until rod on equalizer cylinder extends between $5/16$ inch and $3/4$ inch. Return equalizer valve to "CLOSED" position.

CAUTION

DO NOT OPEN equalizer valve unless flap handle is "UP." Equalization is necessary to insure that flaps will work together.

7. TAXYING INSTRUCTIONS.

Always unlock tail wheel for taxying. Airplane should be turned from side to side to check obstacles. There is no tendency to nose up.

8. TAKE-OFF.

a. PREFLIGHT CHECK.

(1) Trim tabs—Set for take-off. If auxiliary tank is full, set elevator tab $1/4$ inch forward of white mark.

(2) Mixture control—"AUTO-RICH."

(3) Propeller control—"MAX. RPM" (fully forward). Propeller switches — "ON" and "AUTOMATIC."

(4) Fuel selector valve — "MAIN TANK."

(5) Flaps—"UP." (Handle must be left in "UP" position.)

(6) Cowl flaps—"OPEN."

b. TAKE-OFF PROCEDURE.

(1) Turn straight down runway, move straight forward slightly, and "LOCK" tail wheel.

WARNING

Always lock tail wheel prior to take-off. A swing may develop if tail wheel is free.

(2) Half flaps will improve take-off.

(3) Take-off may be made with or without turbine supercharger. To obtain shortest run, supercharger should be used as follows:

(a) Push turbine control "FULL ON" or to setting previously determined to give 52 inches Hg.

(b) Hold with brakes while opening throttle to about 30 inches Hg.

(c) Release brakes and push throttle "FULL ON."

(d) Manifold pressure should not exceed 52 inches Hg.

NOTE

When the interconnected controls are used, the pilot should make certain that the take-off stop is in place. Take-off should be accomplished by pushing all controls (using throttle only) against the stop. It will be necessary to reduce the throttle setting slightly up to 10,000 feet to avoid over-boosting. Above 25,000 feet it may be necessary to go past the stop to obtain military power.

(4) As soon as the airplane is off the ground, move safety latch and raise landing gear lever to "UP." Leave lever at "UP" until it is desired to lower the landing gear. Always complete landing gear cycle except in an emergency. If handle is moved to "UP," allow gear to go completely up before changing handle. If lever is moved to "DN," allow gear to go completely down before changing handle.

9. ENGINE FAILURE DURING TAKE-OFF.

a. Nose down.

b. Landing on field STRAIGHT AHEAD. If too late, retract gear and land OFF field STRAIGHT AHEAD.

CAUTION

DO NOT ATTEMPT TO TURN BACK INTO THE FIELD.

10. CLIMB.

a. Best climbing speed is 140-155 IAS. It will be necessary in prolonged climbs or in hot weather to climb at higher speeds in order to properly cool the engine. Speed of climb should be increased until allowable cylinder head temperature is obtained.

b. Cowl flaps "OPEN." Check cylinder head temperature frequently. If over 260°C (500°F), increase IAS. Check oil temperature (95°C, 203°F) and carburetor air temperature (35°C, 95°F).

11. SUPERCHARGER OPERATION DURING CLIMB AND FLIGHT.

a. The supercharger control should be set so that with full throttle, and supercharger control "FULL ON," 52 inches Hg at 2700 rpm is obtained for take-off. When operating at high power above 7000 feet, the throttle should be wide open and should be left there. Adjustments of power should then be made by the supercharger control. The supercharger control should always be moved slowly, so that manifold pressure will follow and overboost will be avoided.

NOTE

On airplanes equipped with interconnected engine controls, power may be adjusted by operating the throttle only, provided the supercharger and propeller levers are engaged with the throttle.

CAUTION

NEVER shut off throttle completely with the supercharger "ON." Power at altitudes above 27,000 feet is limited by the rpm of the turbine only. Overspeeding of the turbine must be avoided, except in extreme emergencies.

b. NO CARBURETOR FILTER INSTALLED.— Critical altitude at military power (five minutes' operation) is about 27,000 feet. When operating above 27,000 feet in military power, manifold pressure must be reduced 2 inches for each 1000 feet above 27,000. The critical altitude in normal power is about 29,000. When operating above that altitude in normal power, manifold pressure should be reduced 1½ inches Hg for each 1000 feet above 29,000 feet. For example, military power at 40,000 feet is 2700 rpm and 26 inches Hg (for five minutes). Normal power at 40,000 feet is 2550 rpm and 25.5 inches Hg.

CAUTION

NEVER exceed the red line at 18,250 rpm on turbo tachometer except in extreme emergency. ALL OPERATION ABOVE 2230 rpm AND 31 INCHES HG SHOULD BE IN "AUTO-RICH." If carburetor air filter is installed, critical altitude drops to 24,000 feet for military power and to 26,000 feet for normal power. Operation above these altitudes should be restricted as without the air filter above.

12. FLIGHT CHARACTERISTICS.

a. STABILITY.—All models are stable with the rear tank empty. The P-47C-1-RE and subsequent are stable under all loading conditions. The belly tank decreases directional stability. Violent maneuvering or acrobatics should be avoided until belly tank is empty. No high speed diving should be done with fuel in the belly tank.

b. FUEL TANK USE.—Always warm up and take off on "MAIN." Then switch over and RUN OUT BELLY TANK. When no belly tank is installed, always run out rear tank first. While running from either the belly or rear tank, the *main* tank should be switched "ON" for several minutes at intervals to insure that the vented fuel from the carburetor will not cause the main tank to overflow. The amount of vented fuel bypassed to the main tank may be as high as ten U. S. gallons per hour.

c. CHANGE IN TRIM.

(1) The trim tabs are *very* sensitive.

(2) Lowering landing gear—No change.

(3) Lowering flaps—Becomes slightly nose heavy.

(4) Dive—Airplane tends to yaw right as speed increases.

WARNING

Attention is drawn to the fact that on early type airplanes the aileron and rudder trim tab wheels do not work in the same plane as the controls they operate, and that a danger exists that pilots may turn the controls in the wrong direction. Their extreme effectiveness renders this a source of danger, and care must always be exercised to see that the trim tab wheels are rotated in the correct direction to produce the desired effect.

d. ECONOMICAL CRUISING.—Complete engine operating data are contained on the FLIGHT OPERATING INSTRUCTION CHARTS in section III. For economical cruising, set manifold pressure at 28 inches Hg and reduce rpm, depending on the range desired. Low limit for rpm is 1500.

e. ICING CONDITIONS.—Under icing conditions, open carburetor filter bypass, close intercooler shutter, and use higher power with as much turbine supercharger as is consistent. This will result in high carburetor air temperatures and should eliminate the ice.

f. TANK SHIFTING.

(1) When shifting tanks at high altitudes, reduce power and turn on emergency boost while shifting. BE CAREFUL TO STOP ON THE "CLICK."

(2) To shift from auxiliary or main tank to belly tank, place belly tank switch (figure 36-22) in "ON" position first and then place selector valve (figure 16) in "OFF" position.

(3) Due to the fact that the main tank fuel gage is inaccurate at lower readings and that varying amounts of fuel may remain when the tank is run out on "MAIN," a reserve of 10 to 15 gallons should be carried in the auxiliary tank at all times. This fuel can be used at any time that the pilot runs completely out on "MAIN" and "RESERVE." When both tanks are full at take-off, run down to 10 gallons on rear (auxiliary) tank and shift to "MAIN." If the main tank only is to be used, service 10 gallons into auxiliary prior to take-off.

13. ENGINE FAILURE DURING FLIGHT.

a. Nose down.

b. Ignition switch "OFF."

c. If airplane is equipped with a belly tank, pull release lever immediately.

d. Fuel selector valve "OFF."

e. Manually lower flaps.

f. Master battery switch "OFF" (P-47C, P-47D and P-47G only).

g. If a suitable emergency airfield is available, the landing gear may be lowered. IF NOT, KEEP LANDING GEAR "UP" AND LAND AIRPLANE ON ITS BELLY.

14. STALLS.

a. If controls are held in neutral, there is no tendency to spin, although the left wing drops rapidly, and the airplane will dive out and recover.

b. Stalling speeds are as follows:

Flaps and landing gear up—115 mph IAS.
Flaps and landing gear down—100 mph IAS.

c. There is a pronounced tendency for the airplane to snap to the left when stalled in a turn. There is ample warning of the impending stall, however, in the form of buffeting and sloppiness of the controls.

15. SPINS.

a. Spin characteristics of a standard P-47 airplane without belly tank and with a gross weight of approximately 12,500 pounds and a center of gravity location of 28 percent or less are normal, except for a vertical oscillation of the nose during the spin. During all types of maneuvers and spin demonstrations, it has been found that the airplane will never spin of its own accord, but must be forced into the spin by use of elevator and rudder. In order to obtain a stable spin, it is necessary that *full elevator* and *full rudder* be carried at all times. Recovering is made by applying controls in the following sequence:

(1) Full opposite rudder.

(2) Neutral elevators.

(3) Ailerons full against spin.

b. All control movements should be smooth but rapid. The above procedure should give a spin recovery without one-half turn, but in the event it does not, hold controls in this position and apply at least one-half throttle. DO NOT TRY DIFFERENT CONTROL POSITION UNTIL AT LEAST THREE TURNS HAVE BEEN MADE WITH NO CHANGE IN THE SPINNING ATTITUDE. Approximately

1000 feet of altitude will be lost in the entry into the spin, 1000 feet in the recovery and 1000 feet per turn, wheels and flaps up, canopy closed. Approximately 3000 feet per turn is lost with gear down, flaps up. PRACTICE SPINS IN EXCESS OF ½ TURN ARE PROHIBITED.

16. ACROBATICS.

All normal acrobatics are permitted. NO OUTSIDE LOOPS or INVERTED FLIGHT shall be performed. Do not slow roll at speeds over 313 mph IAS. Snap rolls are not recommended and should never be performed above 150 mph IAS.

17. DIVING.

a. Aileron forces become high at speeds above 350 mph IAS. At least 12,000 feet should be allowed for recovery from dives at limiting speed which is 500 mph IAS. NEVER dive with cowl flaps "OPEN."

b. Due to the compressibility effect, diving at high altitude will produce a tendency for the airplane to nose down. If extremely high indicated speeds are reached, the elevator tab will have to be used for recovery. Except in extreme emergencies, an indicated air speed of 400 mph should not be exceeded above 25,000 feet.

18. NIGHT FLYING.

The landing light should be extended only during the final approach and should be left on for the minimum time necessary. Do not extend it at speeds above 200 mph IAS.

CAUTION

BE SURE TO RETRACT LIGHT AT ONCE AFTER TAKE-OFF.

19. EMERGENCY EXIT.

At reasonable speeds, release canopy latch and push canopy to rear. In high speed dive, pull small ring on right forward side of canopy. This will release spoiler flaps on outside of canopy and will assist in moving canopy to rear after releasing latch. Roll airplane on back if possible, push nose up, and pilot will fall clear of all structures (figure 46).

20. APPROACH, LANDING, AND CROSS-WIND LANDING.

a. APPROACH.

(1) Reduce speed to 140-150 mph.

(2) Close cowl flaps.

(3) Mixture control in "AUTO-RICH."

(4) Turbine supercharger "OFF."

(5) Propeller—2550 rpm.

CAUTION

NEVER LOWER LANDING GEAR ABOVE 200 mph.
NEVER LOWER FLAPS ABOVE 195 mph.
NEVER EXCEED 250 mph WITH LANDING GEAR DOWN.

DON'T LOWER YOUR FLAPS
ABOVE 195 MILES PER HOUR

(6) Landing gear and flaps "DOWN." (Flap handle must be left in "DOWN" position.) Check position of gear and flaps on indicator. Check hydraulic pressure. Horn should not blow. If partial flaps are desired, the flap handle should be placed in "NEUTRAL" when the desired position is reached.

(7) Normal approach speeds:

(a) ENGINE "ON"—115-120 mph.

(b) ENGINE "OFF"—120-130 mph.

(8) Do not make steep turns below 130 mph IAS with flaps and landing gear "DOWN."

b. LANDING.

(1) Airplane has no tendency to swing after landing.

(2) Every effort should be made to land on the first quarter of the field. The airplane is heavy and requires considerable distance in which to stop rolling.

c. CROSS-WIND LANDING.—No special comments. Keep airplane straight with runway.

d. EMERGENCY OPERATION OF LANDING GEAR AND FLAPS.—If engine-driven hydraulic pump fails to lower the landing gear or flaps, place the proper handle "DOWN" and manually pump them down. If hand pump fails, place landing gear control

to "DOWN." Landing gear will unlock. Then yaw airplane in both directions until the indicator shows landing gear fully "DOWN" and horn does not blow. Place landing gear control handle in "N" (neutral). Landing gear will remain locked down. If flap system is still intact, flaps can be pumped down by hand.

e. EMERGENCY TAKE-OFF IF LANDING IS NOT COMPLETED.

(1) Open engine to full power, taking care not to exceed 52 inches Hg.

WARNING

Watch the tendency to swing, due to the sudden power application.

(2) Raise landing gear at once.

(3) Open cowl flaps.

(4) Raise flaps when above 500 feet.

(5) DO NOT PULL UP TOO STEEPLY or loss of directional control may result.

21. STOPPING ENGINE.

a. Apply toe brakes and set parking brake lever.

b. When a cold weather start is anticipated, before stopping the engine, hold the oil dilution switch (figure 18-15) in the "ON" position for a period of 4 minutes at 800 rpm. The dilution of the engine oil while the oil temperature is above 70°C (158°F) is not effective. If oil dilution is to be accomplished and oil temperature is too high, stop the engine until it has cooled to 40 to 50°C (104-122°F), restart it and proceed with the oil dilution.

NOTE

At lower temperatures, 4 minutes is inadequate. As much as 8 to 11 minutes may be necessary in two or more periods, 3 to 5 minutes each.

DEVELOP A RUBBER NECK

c. Open engine to 1000 rpm and place mixture control in "IDLE CUT-OFF," holding the dilution switch "ON" until the engine stops.

d. After propeller stops rotating, turn ignition switch "OFF."

22. BEFORE LEAVING PILOT'S COMPARTMENT.

a. Fuel selector valve (figure 16) "OFF."

b. All cockpit light switches, pitot heater switch, generator, master battery switch, etc., "OFF."

c. If oxygen has been used during the flight, close valve to prevent leakage.

d. If windy, lock flight controls to prevent damage to the control surfaces.

23. AIR SPEED CORRECTION.

Mph — IAS	Mph — Calibrated
310	322.5
290	300.5
260	268.5
230	237.5
200	206.5
170	175.0

24. MANEUVERS PROHIBITED.

a. Intentional spins of more than ½ turn.

b. Outside loops.

c. Whip stalls.

d. Inverted flight.

e. Violent maneuvers, practice landings, and high speed dives with belly tank or more than 15 gallons in auxiliary tank.

RESTRICTED

SECTION III
FLIGHT OPERATION DATA

1. GENERAL.

This section presents diagrams and tables containing a summary of specific characteristics, restrictions, and instructions. Every effort has been made to present complete data in simple, practical, and reliable form. Due to limitations of space, the data appear complex but careful study will reveal a surprising amount of valuable information. Distances shown have been adjusted to account for service conditions and are slightly conservative.

2. BALANCE DIAGRAM AND FUSELAGE CONTENTS ARRANGEMENT.

Items of equipment are shown in their relative positions. The numbers in black disks are fuselage stations expressed in inches aft of the nose.

3. WEIGHT AND BALANCE CHART.

Typical loadings are listed, including "Maximum Fuel" for ferrying (with belly tank and ammunition), "Combat" loading with and without "Extra Guns" and ammunition, and "Maximum Load" which includes maximum fuel and armament. A chart is provided to assist in reading proper values on the Take-Off, Climb and Landing Chart.

NOTE

The models vary somewhat and a few have restrictions posted regarding maneuvers. Early models are somewhat lighter and slightly tail heavy.

4. SPECIFIC ENGINE FLIGHT CHART.

Engine limitations and operating characteristics are summarized for ready reference. Learn them! Note restriction when Amend. No. 4 fuel is used.

5. TAKE-OFF, CLIMB, AND LANDING CHART.

a. This chart is a general summary of characteristics with a few pertinent instructions. Note the temperature correction under each table.

b. The following is a sample take-off problem:

Can a P-47G airplane operate from 3,000 feet clearance surrounded by trees if elevation is 2,500 feet, no wind, the surface is sod and the average temperature is about 30°C? Refer to chart. The take-off distance

table under "Sod-Turf Runway," "At 3,000 feet," "To clear 50-foot object" (on account of trees), and opposite 15,000 pounds gross weight and zero wind (top line), reads 4,000 feet; 10% is 400 feet, which must be added for each 10°C above 0°C. For 30°C, three times 400 feet is 1,200 feet, which added to the 4,000 feet gives 5,200 feet required for safe operation. A similar calculation for 12,500 pounds gross shows 130% of 3,200, which is over 4,000 feet. Therefore, use of that field is practically out of the question in spite of the fact that a landing without belly tank could be made in about 2,800 feet with 13,500 pounds gross weight.

c. SAMPLE CLIMB PROBLEM.—With combat loading of eight guns and 1600 rounds of ammunition, what is the minimum time required to climb to 20,000 feet if the estimated air temperature is 15°C? Refer to Weight & Balance Chart. Gross weight is about 13,300 pounds. "Combat" climb to 20,000 feet with 12,500 pounds requires 10.6 minutes and with 14,000 pounds, requires 12.1 minutes; therefore, with 13,300 pounds, the time would be about 11.5 minutes.

6. FLIGHT OPERATION INSTRUCTION CHART.

a. Two charts are provided; sheet 1 applies only until belly tank fuel is exhausted and sheet 2 gives operating instructions for all other loading conditions. The difference is primarily due to the weight of the belly tank fuel.

b. On each chart, note the two reference columns which show gallons of fuel in the upper half of the table and altitudes in the lower half. Other columns are in sets with practical ranges (statute and equivalent nautical air-miles) listed in the upper half, and corresponding operation instructions in the lower half. Progressing from left to right, these columns are arranged to show increase in range at sacrifice in speed with maximum cruising speeds on extreme left and maximum range on extreme right.

c. SAMPLE PROBLEM.—To ferry a P-47G airplane 950 nautical (1100 statute) miles (over water), cruising at 5,000 feet altitude. Reference to the charts indicates that belly tank is required; therefore, flight should be planned in two sections as follows. On sheet 1 find:

(1) Allowing 45 gallons for warm-up, take-off, and climb as noted, 460 gallons (including belly tank) are left for the flight.

(2) The range shown in column IV is 1070 nautical (1230 statute) miles, which gives 120 nautical (140 statute) miles reserve.

(3) Vertically below in the table and opposite 6,000 feet (since 5,000 feet is not listed) reach 2,150 rpm and 225 mph IAS.

(4) Auto-lean mixture must be used since the numbers are in light type.

(5) Turbine waste gate should be open since figures appear below the heavy line (turbine to be used for cruising P-47 airplanes only with full throttle, except when using turbine is necessary to prevent or eliminate icing of the carburetor). These conditions should be re-established hourly until all fuel has been used from the belly tank. For the balance of the flight, reference to column IV of sheet 2 indicates that the rpm should be decreased to 1,950 and the indicated speed set hourly at 230 mph. As indicated by the charts, no change in mixture or supercharger controls is required.

d. As an alternate plan, reference to column on the extreme right of each chart shows that for maximum range the flight may be made with a decrease of 25 to 30 mph if 320 nautical (370 statute) miles reserve is desired. This will result in about a half-hour increase in flight time.

e. If on the first flight described above with 250 gallons remaining, a fix is obtained indicating 500 nautical (580 statute) miles yet to go and weather makes flight at 15,000 feet necessary, reference to the table on sheet 2 indicates that the best conditions are 2100 rpm (full throttle) with turbo set to give 220 mph indicated air speed, and auto-lean mixture. These conditions indicate a reserve of over 100 miles, which was originally planned.

NOTE

RANGES LISTED in column on extreme right should not be attempted with these airplanes above 13,500 feet altitude.

WARNING FOR THE TROPICS

Hot gas at take-off may reduce range as much as 10 percent. Make allowance!

FLIGHT OPERATION INSTRUCTION CHART

MODEL (S) P-47 SERIES
SOME EARLY MODELS HAVE NO PROVISIONS FOR BELLY...

EXTERNAL LOAD ITEMS
200-GAL. BELLY TANK

SHEET 1 OF 2 SHEETS

GR. WT. 15,000 TO 13,500 POUNDS

CONDITION	R.P.M.	M.P. (IN. HG)	BLOWER POSITION	MIXTURE POSITION	DURATION IN MIN.	U.S. G.P.H.	IMP. G.P.H.
TAKE-OFF	2700	52		A.R.	5		
MILITARY POWER	2700	52		A.R.	5		

ENGINE (S) R-2800-21 (WITH TURBO)

INSTRUCTIONS FOR USING CHART: Select figure in fuel column equal to or less than total amount of fuel in airplane. Move horizontally to the right or left and select a figure equal to or greater than the air miles to be flown. Vertically below and opposite desired cruising altitude read optimum cruising conditions. **NOTES:** (A) Avoid continuous cruising in Column I except in emergency. (B) Columns (II, III, IV & V) toward the right progressively give increase in range at sacrifice in speed. (C) Manifold Pressure (M.P.), Gallons Per Hour (G.P.H.), are approximate maximum values for reference. (D) For quick reference, take-off and military power data are listed in the upper left corner of chart.

ALTERNATE CRUISING CONDITIONS (NO RESERVE FUEL ALLOWANCE)

I (MAX. CONT. POWER) (NO WIND)

RANGE IN AIR MILES — STATUTE	NAUTICAL	FUEL U.S. GALS	DENSITY ALT. IN FEET
750	650	505	30000
890	800	480	25000
850	580	425	20000
810	530	400	15000
580	500	375	12000
540	470	350	9000
500	430	325	6000
		300	3000
			S.L.

(Continued on sheet 2)

I — OPERATING DATA

R.P.M.	T.A.S. KNOTS	T.A.S. M.P.H.	M.P. IN. HG	U.S. G.P.H.	IMP. G.P.H.
2550	325	283	37	190	158
2550	305	265	36	180	150
2550	295	257	36	175	146
2550	285	248	35	170	142
2550	270	235	35	160	133
2550	260	226	36	155	129
2550	255	222	37	150	125

II

RANGE IN AIR MILES — STATUTE	NAUTICAL
920 (45 U.S.)	800 (38 IMP.)
850	740
810	700
760	660
710	610
660	570
620	540

(Continued on sheet 2)

II — OPERATING DATA

R.P.M.	I.A.S. KNOTS	I.A.S. M.P.H.	M.P. IN. HG	U.S. G.P.H.	IMP. G.P.H.
2550	210	183	35	160	133
2550	215	187	34	150	125
2500	220	191	32	140	117
2450	225	196	32	135	112
2400	230	200	32	130	108

USE COLUMN IV BELOW 12,000 FT. ALT.

III

GALLONS NOT AVAILABLE IN FLIGHT

IV

RANGE IN AIR MILES — STATUTE	NAUTICAL	FUEL IMP. GALS	DENSITY ALT. IN FEET
1230	1070	421	30000
1140	990	383	25000
1080	930	354	20000
1020	880	334	15000
980	830	312	12000
900	780	292	9000
840	730	271	6000
		250	3000
			S.L.

(Continued on Sheet 2)

IV — OPERATING DATA

R.P.M.	I.A.S. KNOTS	I.A.S. M.P.H.	M.P. IN. HG	U.S. G.P.H.	IMP. G.P.H.
2250	180	157	32	110	92
2200	190	165	32	105	87
2250	205	178	32	105	87
2200	215	187	32	100	83
2200	220	191	32	100	83
2200	225	196	32	95	79
2150	225	196	33	90	75
2100	230	200	35	90	75
2050	230	200	36	85	71

V (MAX. RANGE)

RANGE IN AIR MILES — STATUTE	NAUTICAL
1470	1270
1370	1190
1300	1130
1220	1060
1150	1000
1070	930
1000	870

V — OPERATING DATA

R.P.M.	I.A.S. M.P.H.	I.A.S. KNOTS	M.P. IN. HG	U.S. G.P.H.	IMP. G.P.H.
1900	200	174	32	75	63
1900	200	174	31	70	58
1750	200	174	33	70	58
1700	200	174	34	65	54
1650	205	178	35	60	50

① INDICATED ALTITUDE CORRECTED FOR FREE AIR TEMPERATURE.
② ALLOW 45 U.S. GALS. 38 IMP. GALS. FOR WARM UP, TAKE-OFF AND CLIMB TO 5,000 FEET ALTITUDE
③ RETURN FUEL FLOWS TO TANK.

USE FUEL FROM TANKS IN THE FOLLOWING ORDER.

REFER TO "SPECIFIC ENGINE FLIGHT CHART" FOR ADDITIONAL ENGINE OPERATION DATA.

BOLD NUMBERS: Use Auto-Rich
LIGHT NUMBERS: Use Auto-Lean
WITH TWO SPEED BLOWER: Use Turbo blower above heavy line only

I.A.S.: Indicated Air Speed
M.P.: Manifold Pressure (In. Hg.)
U.S.G.P.H.: U.S. Gallons Per Hour
IMP.G.P.H.: Imperial Gallons Per Hour
F.T.: Full Throttle

EDITOR'S NOTE: AAF inspectors at modification centers will strike out columns not matching calibration of instruments in the airplane at time of delivery.

RED FIGURES ARE PRELIMINARY; SUBJECT TO REVISION AFTER FLIGHT CHECK

MODEL (S)	FLIGHT OPERATION INSTRUCTION CHART	EXTERNAL LOAD ITEMS
P-47B, P-47C (EST.) P-47D (EST.) AND P-47G	SHEET 2 OF 2 SHEETS GR. WT. 13,500 TO 11,000 POUNDS	NONE-OR EMPTY 200-GAL. BELLY TANK

CONDITION	R.P.M.	M.P. (IN. HG)	BLOWER POSITION	MIXTURE POSITION	DURATION IN MIN.	U.S. G.P.H.	IMP. G.P.H.
TAKE-OFF	2700	52		A.R.	5		
MILITARY POWER	2700	52		A.R.	5		
ENGINE (S)	R-2800-21 (WITH TURBO)						

INSTRUCTIONS FOR USING CHART: Select figure in fuel column equal to or less than total amount of fuel in airplane. Move horizontally to the right or left and select a figure equal to or greater than the air miles to be flown. Vertically below and opposite desired cruising altitude read optimum cruising conditions. NOTES: (A) Avoid continuous cruising in Column I except in emergency. (B) Columns (II, III, IV & V) toward the right progressively give increase in range at sacrifice in speed. (C) Manifold Pressure (M.P.), Gallons Per Hour (G.P.H.), are approximate maximum values for reference. (D) For quick reference, take-off and military power data are listed in the upper left corner of chart.

ALTERNATE CRUISING CONDITIONS

(NO WIND) (NO RESERVE FUEL ALLOWANCE)

I (MAX. CONT. POWER) Range in Air Miles: Statute	I Nautical	FUEL U.S. GALS. (2)	II Statute	II Nautical	III Statute	III Nautical	IV Statute	IV Nautical	FUEL IMP. GALS. (2)	V (MAX. RANGE) Statute	V Nautical
		305	40 U.S. (33 IMP.) GALLONS NOT AVAILABLE IN FLIGHT						254		
450	390	265	550	475			750	640	221	880	760
430	370	250	515	450			700	605	208	830	715
385	330	225	465	405			625	545	188	750	640
340	295	200	415	360			555	485	167	665	570
300	265	175	360	315			485	425	146	580	500
255	220	150	310	270			415	360	125	500	430
210	185	125	260	225			345	300	108	415	355
170	145	100	205	180			275	240	83	330	285
125	110	75	155	135			210	180	63	250	215
85	75	50	100	90			140	120	42	165	140
40	35	25	50	45			70	60	21	80	70

OPERATING DATA — Column I

DENSITY ALT. IN FEET (1)	R.P.M.	T.A.S. M.P.H.	T.A.S. KNOTS	M.P. IN. HG	U.S. G.P.H.	IMP. G.P.H.
30000	2550	370	322	36	205	171
25000	2500	360	314	38	190	158
20000	2450	330	287	37	175	146
15000	2450	310	270	36	165	138
12000	2400	300	261	35	160	133
9000	2400	285	248	34	150	125
6000	2350	275	239	34	145	121
3000	2350	265	231	35	140	117
S.L.	2350	255	222	36	135	112

OPERATING DATA — Columns II and III

DENSITY ALT. IN FEET (1)	II R.P.M.	II I.A.S. M.P.H.	II I.A.S. KNOTS	II M.P. IN. HG	II U.S. G.P.H.	II IMP. G.P.H.	III R.P.M.	III I.A.S. M.P.H.	III I.A.S. KNOTS	III M.P. IN. HG	III U.S. G.P.H.	III IMP. G.P.H.
30000	2350	210	183	35	150	125						
25000	2350	225	196	36	145	121						
20000	2300	225	196	34	135	112						
15000	2300	230	200	32	125	104						
12000	2250	235	205	32	120	100						
9000												
6000	USE COLUMN IV											
3000	BELOW 12,000 FEET											
S.L.												

OPERATING DATA — Columns IV and V

DENSITY ALT. IN FEET (1)	IV R.P.M.	IV I.A.S. M.P.H.	IV I.A.S. KNOTS	IV M.P. IN. HG	IV U.S. G.P.H.	IV IMP. G.P.H.	V R.P.M.	V I.A.S. M.P.H.	V I.A.S. KNOTS	V M.P. IN. HG	V U.S. G.P.H.	V IMP. G.P.H.
30000	2150	190	165	32	100	83						
25000	2150	200	174	31	95	79						
20000	2150	210	183	30	95	79						
15000	2100	220	191	32	90	75						
12000	2050	225	196	33	85	71	1750	200	174	32	65	54
9000	2050	230	200	32	85	71	1800	205	178	30	65	54
6000	1950	230	200	34	80	67	1700	205	178	31	60	50
3000	1950	230	200	35	80	67	1700	200	174	32	55	46
S.L.	1950	235	205	35	75	63	1700	200	174	32	55	46

LEGEND

(1) INDICATED ALTITUDE CORRECTED FOR FREE AIR TEMPERATURE.
(2) ALLOW 45 U.S. GALS. 38 IMP. GALS FOR WARM UP.
TAKE-OFF AND CLIMB TO 5,000 FEET ALTITUDE
RETURN FUEL FLOWS TO TANK
USE FUEL FROM TANKS IN THE FOLLOWING ORDER

BOLD NUMBERS: Use Auto-Rich
LIGHT NUMBERS: Use Auto-Lean
WITH TWO SPEED BLOWER: Use Turbo blower above heavy line only

I.A.S.: Indicated Air Speed
M.P.: Manifold Pressure (In. Hg.)
U.S.G.P.H.: U.S. Gallons Per Hour
IMP.G.P.H.: Imperial Gallons Per Hour
F.T.: Full Throttle

EDITOR'S NOTE: AAF inspectors at modification centers will strike out columns not matching calibration of instruments in the airplane at time of delivery.

REFER TO "SPECIFIC ENGINE FLIGHT CHART" FOR ADDITIONAL ENGINE OPERATION DATA.

RED FIGURES ARE PRELIMINARY: SUBJECT TO REVISION AFTER FLIGHT CHECK

SPECIFIC ENGINE FLIGHT CHART

AIRPLANE MODELS P-47 SERIES

ENGINE MODELS R-2800-21

CONDITION	FUEL PRESSURE LB/SQ.IN.	OIL PRESSURE LB/SQ.IN.	OIL TEMP. °C	COOLANT TEMP. °C
DESIRED	16-17	75-85	50-70	
MAXIMUM	17	90	95	
MINIMUM	16	60	40	
IDLING	7	25		

SUPERCHARGER TYPE: TURBINE

MAX. PERMISSIBLE DIVING R.P.M. 3050

CONDITION	ALLOWABLE OIL CONSUMPTION
"MAX CONTINUOUS"	55 IMP PT/HR. 33 U.S.QT/HR.
"ECONOMICAL MAX"	35 IMP PT/HR. 21 U.S.QT/HR.
"MIN. SPECIFIC"	22 IMP PT/HR. 13 U.S.QT/HR.
OIL GRADE:	(S) 1120 (W) 1100A

FUEL OCTANE "100 (AMEND. #5)

OPERATING CONDITION	R.P.M.	MANIF. PRESS. (BOOST)	HORSE POWER	CRITICAL ALTITUDE (FEET)	BLOWER	USE LOW BLOWER BELOW	MIXTURE CONTROL POSITION	FUEL FLOW (GAL./HR./ENG.) U.S.	IMP.	MAXIMUM CYL. TEMP. °C	°F	MAXIMUM DURATION (MINUTES)	REMARKS
TAKE-OFF	2700	52"	2000				AUTO-RICH	275	229	260	500	5	TURBINE REQUIRED FOR TAKE-OFF
EMERGENCY MAXIMUM	2700	52"	2000	27,000		FT. ALT.	A.R.	275	229	260	500	5	REDUCE MANIF. PRESS. 2" HG PER 1000 FT. ABOVE 27,000 FT.
MAXIMUM CONTINUOUS	2550	42	1625	29,000	SINGLE SPEED	FT. ALT.	A.R.	210	175	232	450	NO LIMIT	REDUCE MANIF. PRESS. 1½" HG PER 1000 FT. ABOVE 29000 FT.
ECONOMICAL MAXIMUM	2250	32	1200	25,000		FT. ALT.	AUTO-LEAN	105	88	232	450	NO LIMIT	AVOID TURBINE BOOST WITH PART THROTTLE
MINIMUM SPECIFIC CONSUMPTION	1700	32	800	5,000			A.L.	60	50	232	450		TURBINE BOOST SHOULD NOT BE REQUIRED BELOW 12,000 FT.
	1850	31	950	15,000			A.L.	70	58	232	450		
	2150	31	1100	25,000		FT. ALT.	A.L.	95	79	232	450		
MINIMUM CRUISING	1600			S.L. TO 25,000		FT. ALT.	A.L.			232	450		

CONDITIONS

1. IF NO TURBINE TACHOMETER IS INSTALLED OBSERVE RULES IN "REMARKS" COLUMN TO AVOID OVERSPEEDING TURBINE IF TURBINE TACH. IS INSTALLED DO NOT EXCEED 18,250 TURBINE R.P.M.
2. IF CARB. AIR TEMP. EXCEEDS 35° C WITH INTERCOOLER DOORS OPEN DO NOT EXCEED 2550 R.P.M. & 42" HG.
   * MANIFOLD PRESSURE MUST NOT EXCEED 47" HG IF FUEL IS 100 OCTANE (AMEND. #4).

TO AVOID

NOTE: CRITICAL ALTITUDE IS THAT AT WHICH MAXIMUM POWER IS OBTAINED WITH FULL THROTTLE UNDER CONDITIONS SHOWN.

5-1-42

AIRPLANE MODELS P-47 SERIES — TAKE-OFF, CLIMB & LANDING CHART — ENGINE MODELS R-2800-21

TAKE-OFF DISTANCE (IN FEET)

HARD SURFACE RUNWAY

GROSS WEIGHT (IN LBS.)	HEAD WIND (MPH)	AT SEA LEVEL GROUND RUN	AT SEA LEVEL TO CLEAR 50' OBJ	AT 3,000 FT. GROUND RUN	AT 3,000 FT. TO CLEAR 50' OBJ	AT 6,000 FT. GROUND RUN	AT 6,000 FT. TO CLEAR 50' OBJ
15,000	0	2400	3500	2600	3800	2900	4200
	20	1800	2600	2000	3000	2200	3300
	40	1200	1800	1400	2000	1600	2300
14,000	0	2100	3100	2300	3400	2500	3800
	20	1500	2200	1700	2600	1900	2900
	40	1000	1500	1200	1800	1400	2100
12,500	0	1800	2800	2000	3100	2200	3400
	20	1300	2000	1500	2300	1600	2500
	40	900	1400	1000	1500	1200	1800

SOD-TURF RUNWAY

GROSS WEIGHT (IN LBS.)	HEAD WIND (MPH)	AT SEA LEVEL GROUND RUN	AT SEA LEVEL TO CLEAR 50' OBJ	AT 3,000 FT. GROUND RUN	AT 3,000 FT. TO CLEAR 50' OBJ	AT 6,000 FT. GROUND RUN	AT 6,000 FT. TO CLEAR 50' OBJ
15,000	0	2500	3600	2800	4000	3000	4300
	20	1900	2700	2100	3100	2300	3400
	40	1300	1900	1500	2100	1700	2400
14,000	0	2200	3200	2400	3500	2600	3900
	20	1600	2300	1800	2700	2000	3000
	40	1100	1600	1300	1900	1500	2200
12,500	0	1900	2900	2100	3200	2300	3500
	20	1400	2100	1600	2400	1700	2600
	40	1000	1500	1100	1600	1300	1900

SOFT SURFACE RUNWAY

GROSS WEIGHT (IN LBS.)	HEAD WIND (MPH)	AT SEA LEVEL GROUND RUN	AT SEA LEVEL TO CLEAR 50' OBJ	AT 3,000 FT. GROUND RUN	AT 3,000 FT. TO CLEAR 50' OBJ	AT 6,000 FT. GROUND RUN	AT 6,000 FT. TO CLEAR 50' OBJ
15,000	0	2800	3900	3000	4200	3300	4600
	20	2100	2900	2300	3300	2500	3600
	40	1400	2000	1600	2300	1800	2500
14,000	0	2400	3400	2600	3700	2900	4200
	20	1800	2500	2000	2900	2200	3200
	40	1200	1700	1400	2000	1600	2300
12,500	0	2100	3100	2300	3400	2500	3700
	20	1600	2300	1700	2500	1900	2800
	40	1100	1600	1400	1700	1400	2000

NOTE: INCREASE DISTANCE 10% FOR EACH 10°C ABOVE 0°C

ENGINE LIMITS FOR TAKE-OFF   2700 RPM & 52 IN. HG

CLIMB DATA

COMBAT MISSIONS USE *2700 RPM & 52 IN. HG   FERRY MISSIONS USE 2350 RPM & 35 IN. HG

GROSS WEIGHT (IN LBS.)	TYPE OF CLIMB	S.L. TO 5000 FT. ALT. BEST I.A.S.	S.L. TO 5000 FT. ALT. FT./MIN.	S.L. TO 5000 FT. ALT. TIME FROM S.L.	AT 10,000 FT. ALT. FT./MIN.	AT 10,000 FT. ALT. BEST I.A.S.	AT 10,000 FT. ALT. TIME FROM S.L.	AT 10,000 FT. ALT. FUEL FROM S.L.	AT 15,000 FT. ALT. FT./MIN.	AT 15,000 FT. ALT. BEST I.A.S.	AT 15,000 FT. ALT. TIME FROM S.L.	AT 15,000 FT. ALT. FUEL FROM S.L.	AT 20,000 FT. ALT. FT./MIN.	AT 20,000 FT. ALT. BEST I.A.S.	AT 20,000 FT. ALT. TIME FROM S.L.	AT 20,000 FT. ALT. FUEL FROM S.L.	AT 25,000 FT. ALT. FT./MIN.	AT 25,000 FT. ALT. BEST I.A.S.	AT 25,000 FT. ALT. TIME FROM S.L.	AT 25,000 FT. ALT. FUEL FROM S.L.	BLOWER CHANGE
15,000	COMBAT	165	1850	3	1350	165	6	60	1200	155	10	75	1000	155	14	90	900	155	19	110	
	FERRY	165	750	7	750	165	14	70	700	155	21	90	600	155	28	110	500	155	37	135	
14,000	COMBAT	165	2050	2.4	2050	165	4.9	57	1400	155	8.3	70	1250	155	12.1	83	1050	155	16.4	98	
	FERRY	165	850	6	850	165	12	65	800	155	18	85	750	155	25	100	600	155	32	120	
12,500	COMBAT	165	2300	2.2	2300	165	4.4	55	1550	155	7.2	66	1400	155	10.6	78	1250	155	14.5	91	
	FERRY	165	1000	5	1000	165	10	60	950	155	15	75	900	155	21	90	800	155	27	105	

NOTE: INCREASED ELAPSED CLIMBING TIME 10% FOR EACH 10°C ABOVE 0°C FREE AIR TEMPERATURE

FUEL INCLUDES WARM-UP AND TAKE-OFF ALLOWANCE

LANDING DISTANCE (IN FEET)

GROSS WEIGHT (IN LBS.)	BEST I.A.S. Approach	HARD DRY SURFACE AT SEA LEVEL TO CLEAR 50' OBJ	HARD DRY SURFACE AT SEA LEVEL GROUND ROLL	HARD DRY SURFACE AT 3,000 FT. TO CLEAR 50' OBJ	HARD DRY SURFACE AT 3,000 FT. GROUND ROLL	HARD DRY SURFACE AT 6,000 FT. TO CLEAR 50' OBJ	HARD DRY SURFACE AT 6,000 FT. GROUND ROLL	FIRM DRY SOD AT SEA LEVEL TO CLEAR 50' OBJ	FIRM DRY SOD AT SEA LEVEL GROUND ROLL	FIRM DRY SOD AT 3,000 FT. TO CLEAR 50' OBJ	FIRM DRY SOD AT 3,000 FT. GROUND ROLL	FIRM DRY SOD AT 6,000 FT. TO CLEAR 50' OBJ	FIRM DRY SOD AT 6,000 FT. GROUND ROLL	WET OR SLIPPERY AT SEA LEVEL TO CLEAR 50' OBJ	WET OR SLIPPERY AT SEA LEVEL GROUND ROLL	WET OR SLIPPERY AT 3,000 FT. TO CLEAR 50' OBJ	WET OR SLIPPERY AT 3,000 FT. GROUND ROLL	WET OR SLIPPERY AT 6,000 FT. TO CLEAR 50' OBJ	WET OR SLIPPERY AT 6,000 FT. GROUND ROLL
13,500	130	2400	1550	2600	1700	2800	1850	2600	1750	2800	1900	3000	2050	4500	3650	4900	4000	5300	4350
10,600	115	2000	1200	2200	1400	2300	1500	2100	1300	2300	1500	2500	1700	3600	2800	3900	3100	4200	3400

NOTE: FOR GROUND TEMPERATURES ABOVE 35°C (95°F) INCREASE APPROACH I.A.S. 10% AND ALLOW 20% INCREASE IN GROUND ROLL.

REMARKS: * FOR COMBAT CLIMB, REDUCE TO 2550 RPM AND 42 "HG WITHIN 5 MINUTES FROM START OF TAKE-OFF. IF 100 OCTANE (AMEND. #4) FUEL IS BEING USED, DO NOT EXCEED 47" HG. FOR TAKE-OFF OR CLIMB.

LEGEND

I. A. S.: Indicated Air Speed

NOTE: All distances are average, and subject to considerable variations because of differences in pilot technique, load, C.G., etc.

RED FIGURES HAVE NOT BEEN FLIGHT CHECKED.

11-20-42

WEIGHT & BALANCE CHART

AIRPLANE MODELS		BALANCE (C.G.) LIMITS		
P-47 SERIES	P-47B IS ABOUT 200 LB. LIGHTER AND DOES NOT CARRY A BELLY TANK	CONDITION	PERCENT M.A.C.	
		TAKE-OFF	25 % TO 32 %	
		LANDING	25 % TO 32 %	

BASIC LOAD ITEMS	POUNDS
WEIGHT EMPTY, (INCLUDING : SCR-274-N OR SCR-522-A RADIO)	9912
FIXED GUN INSTALLATION (S): (6) .50 CAL 430 LB ( ) ___ CAL ___ LB GUN SIGHT 2 LB	
FIXED CANNON INSTALLATION(S): ( ) ___ MM ___ LB ( ) ___ MM ___ LB	
FLEXIBLE GUN INSTALLATION(S): ( ) ___ CAL ___ LB ( ) ___ CAL ___ LB	
FLEXIBLE CANNON INSTALLATION (S) ( ) ___ MM ___ LB ( ) ___ MM ___ LB	432
EQUIPMENT : NAVIGATION -- LB PHOTOGRAPHIC -- LB OXYGEN 7 LB	
PYROTECNICS (FLARES ETC) 6 LB	13
CREW 1 (200 LB EA INCLUDING PARACHUTES) 200 LB OIL (19.1 US GAL 15.9 IMP GALL) 143 LB.	343
TACTICAL WEIGHT EMPTY (C.G. 27 % M A C.)	10700

ALTERNATE ITEMS			ALTERNATE LOADING (POUNDS)			
			MAXIMUM FUEL	NORMAL COMBAT	SPECIAL COMBAT	MAXIMUM LOAD
FUEL (6 LB PER US GAL - 7.2 LB PER IMPERIAL GALL)	US GAL	(IMP GALL)				
MAIN FUEL TANK (FORWARD)	205	(171)	1230	1230	1230	1230
AUX. FUEL TANK (AFT.)	100	(83)	600		600	600
		(___)				
BELLY TANK	200	(166)	1200			1200
(NOTE: NO PROVISIONS FOR BELLY		(___)				
TANK ON P-47B)		(___)				
EXTRA TANK (S) INSTALLATION 200 GAL. BELLY TANK			133			133
EXTRA OIL (AS REQUIRED - MAXIMUM IS SHOWN) 9.6 G (8.0)			72		72	72
BOMB INSTALLATION (S): INTERNAL ( ) ___ LB						
( ) EXTERNAL ___ LB OR ( ) EXTERNAL ___ LB						
TORPEDO INSTALLATION						
ALTERNATE FIXED GUN INSTALLATION: - 2 - .50 CAL.			--	--	145	145
AMMUNITION : 1800 RDS .50 CAL (OR) 1200 RDS .50 CAL			360	540	360	--
MAX. 3400 RDS .50 CAL. ___ RDS ___ MM			--	--	--	1020
FOR ALTERNATE GUNS - 400 RDS. .50 CAL.			--	--	120	--
PASSENGERS ___ BAGGAGE (MAX) ___ LB						
MISC.			5	30	73	
TACTICAL WEIGHT EMPTY			10700	10700	10700	10700
GROSS WEIGHT			14300	12500	13300	15000
NOTE: 1% M A C = .87 INCHES BALANCE (IN PERCENT M.A.C.)			31	28	29	31

RESTRICTED

SECTION IV
COMMUNICATIONS EQUIPMENT

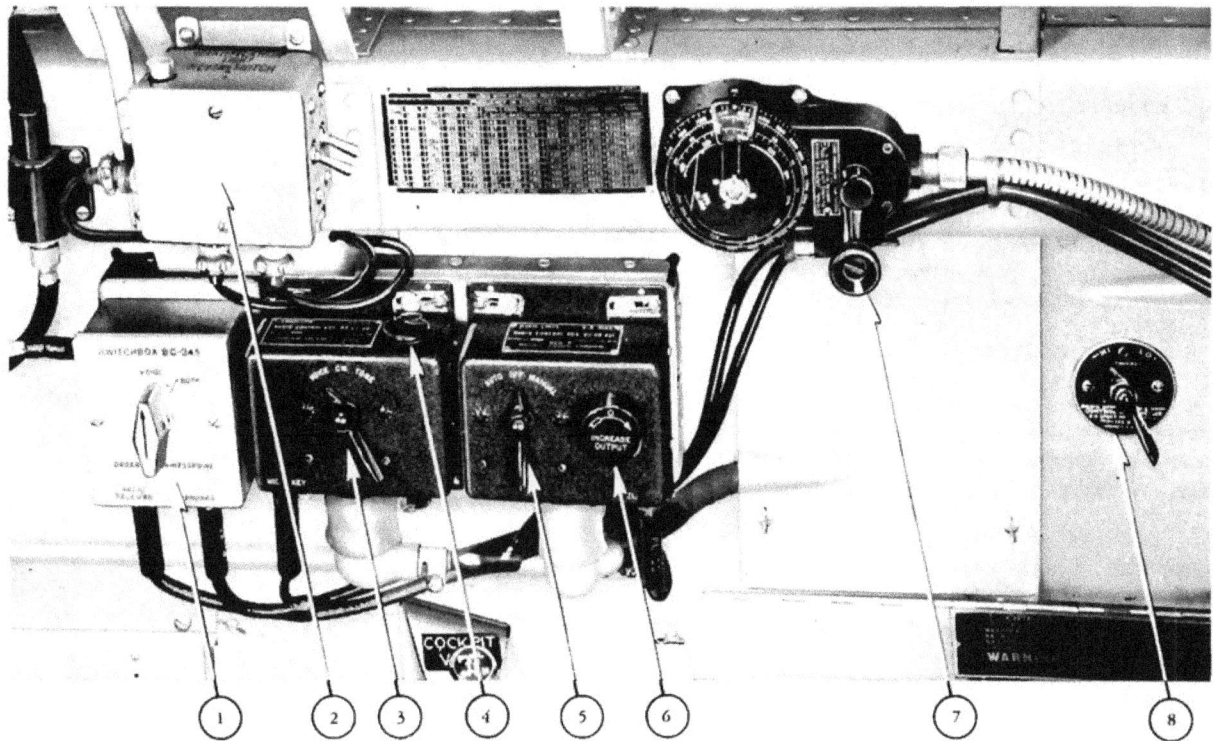

1. Crystal Filter Selector Switch
2. Identification Light Switches
3. Transmitter Emission Control Switch
4. Transmitting Key
5. Radio Receiver Volume Control Selector Switch
6. Receiver Off-On Volume Control
7. Tuning Dial Control Crank
8. Radio Receiver "Hi-Lo" Switch

Figure 36—Radio Controls, P-47B

1. P-47B AIRPLANE.

a. GENERAL DESCRIPTION.

(1) INSTALLATION. — The radio installation consists of a type SCR-283 command set equipped with a range filter and a throat microphone. A "push-to-talk" button is provided on the engine throttle, with all other operating controls located on the right side of the cockpit.

(2) RECEIVER.—The receiver is calibrated and adjusted to receive the radio range frequencies between 201 and 398 kilocycles, and the tactical communication range between 2500 and 7700 kilocycles. Provisions for receiving other frequencies can be installed by a radio technician.

(3) TRANSMITTER.

(*a*) The transmitter will operate on any frequency between 2500 and 7700 kilocycles at which the radio technician sets it. It is capable of transmitting voice, modulated CW (MCW), or straight CW signals.

(*b*) The effective range of the transmitter for dependable voice transmission is approximately 25 miles.

b. OPERATING INSTRUCTIONS.

(1) RECEIVER.

(*a*) Turn receiver control box selector switch (figure 36-5) on "MANUAL." Plug receiver phones in jack number JK-26 and turn volume control knob (figure 36-6) to the right until a frying noise or a signal is heard in the head set.

CAUTION

For all normal (voice or MCW) reception, the radio receiver crystal filter selector switch should be set at "BOTH." To receive the radio range "MCW" without possibility of voice interference, set the selector switch to "RANGE." To receive voice without possibility of radio range interference, set the selector switch to "VOICE." IT IS IMPOSSIBLE TO RECEIVE VOICE WHEN THIS SELECTOR SWITCH IS SET ON "RANGE."

(*b*) To receive the radio ranges and control tower on 201 to 398 kilocycles, set the "HI-LO" selector switch (figure 36-8) to "LO." Adjust tuning dial knob for desired frequency as calibrated on the inner scale of tuning dial.

NOTE

When tuning receiver for a definite frequency, always turn dial a little to each side of the calibration mark to find the point where the signal is strongest. This procedure is to be followed when the receiver selector switch is set on "MANUAL."

(*c*) To receive tactical frequencies, turn the "HI-LO" selector switch to "HI." Adjust tuning dial knob for desired frequency as calibrated on the outer scale of the tuning dial. The intermediate scale on the tuning dial (0-100 scale) is used only in special instances when special frequency ranges are being used, and require installation of special coils by radio maintenance personnel. In this case, there will be found a metal "FREQUENCY IN KC" calibration chart installed in every cockpit near the tuning dial.

NOTE

THE "HI-LO" selector switch is connected to the receiver by a spring cable and must be operated by the "click and feel" method. Care must be taken to insure proper contact in either "HI" or "LO" position, since the position of the pointer does not accurately indicate the setting.

(*d*) TO RECEIVE CODE.

1. Straight continuous wave signals (CW) cannot be heard on this receiver, as it is not equipped with a beat frequency oscillator.

2. Tone (MCW) signals may be heard on this receiver by tuning in the same manner as for voice reception with the radio range filter selector switch set on "BOTH."

(*e*) The receiver (and transmitter filaments) may be turned off by placing the control box selector switch in its "OFF" position.

(2) TRANSMITTER.

(*a*) Place throat microphone around neck and adjust the band so that its two circular elements are held snugly against each side of the throat just *above* the "adam's-apple."

(*b*) Before transmitting, adjust radio receiver to the same frequency as the station with which you desire to talk, and listen in to be sure the operator is not talking to someone else. If the station is transmitting, take advantage of the opportunity to more accurately set the airplane receiver on the assigned frequency, and when the other operator is through, proceed with your transmission.

(c) VOICE TRANSMISSION.

1. Set transmitter emission selector switch (figure 36-3) to "VOICE."

2. When the selector switch is set on "AUTO" or "MANUAL," press the microphone button located on the engine throttle and start talking. Speak *slowly, distinctly,* and in a *normal* tone of voice. Shouting will seriously distort the voice signal.

3. Release the microphone button when through talking.

(d) CODE TRANSMISSION.

1. TONE (MCW).—Set transmitter emission selector switch (figure 36-3) to "TONE" and operate transmitter key (figure 36-4).

2. CW. — Set transmitter emission selector switch to "CW" and operate transmitter key.

NOTE

Any receiving station "standing by" a particular frequency, expecting voice signals, will hear any "TONE" (MCW) code transmissions. However, this station will not hear "CW" signals unless his receiver is equipped with a beat frequency oscillator, and the oscillator is turned on. Ground stations and bomber airplanes are usually equipped with receivers containing a beat frequency oscillator. Fighter airplanes are not equipped to receive "CW" signals.

c. OPERATION NOTES FOR PILOT.

(1) UNABLE TO RECEIVE.

(a) Ascertain that receiver selector switch is on "MANUAL" or "AUTO."

(b) Ascertain that the "HI-LO" switch is in proper position and is making good contact. Refer to NOTE under paragraph 1.*b.*(1)*(c).* Test receiver operation on band known to be in use.

(c) Systematically check for secure connections in all cables and wires about the radio controls, starting with head set and ending at the receiver control box.

(d) Turn range filter switch pointer to all positions to be sure internal contact points are making good connection, or that the pointer is not set somewhere between positions.

(e) Turn volume control through its entire range to test for an intermittent short circuit or some isolated position where receiver is inoperative.

(2) UNABLE TO TRANSMIT.

(a) Ascertain that receiver (and transmitter filament) selector switch is set on "MANUAL" or "AUTO."

(b) Be sure that the transmitter emission selector switch is not set between positions.

(c) Carefully inspect microphone for evidence of damage due to rough treatment.

(d) Systematically check for secure connections in all cables and wires about the radio controls, starting with the microphone and ending at the transmitter control box.

(e) If transmitter does not "come on" for voice transmission when the "push-to-talk" button on the engine throttle is operated, hold the transmitter key down; operate the "push-to-talk" button if failure was on "TONE" or "CW."

NOTE

The key and "push-to-talk" button may be substituted for each other for any three positions of the transmitter emission control.

2. P-47C, P-47D, and P-47G AIRPLANES.

a. GENERAL.—Provisions are made for the installation of either the SCR-274N or the SCR-522A radio set in these airplanes. The contractor, RC-96 (pip squeak), is used in conjunction with either of the two command sets. The command radio equipment is located in the baggage compartment (figure 29-17) and is accessible through the baggage compartment door. All radio equipment is controlled remotely by the pilot through control boxes located on the right side of the cockpit.

b. COMMAND SET SCR-274N.

(1) DESCRIPTION.—The command set SCR-274N is designed for communicating with nearby aircraft for tactical purposes and with ground stations for navigational and traffic control purposes. Three receivers and one transmitter are installed in the rear of the fuselage. All dials and controls are located on remote control units to the right of the pilot.

(2) RECEIVING.

(a) The receiver remote control unit is divided into three identical sections, each section controlling

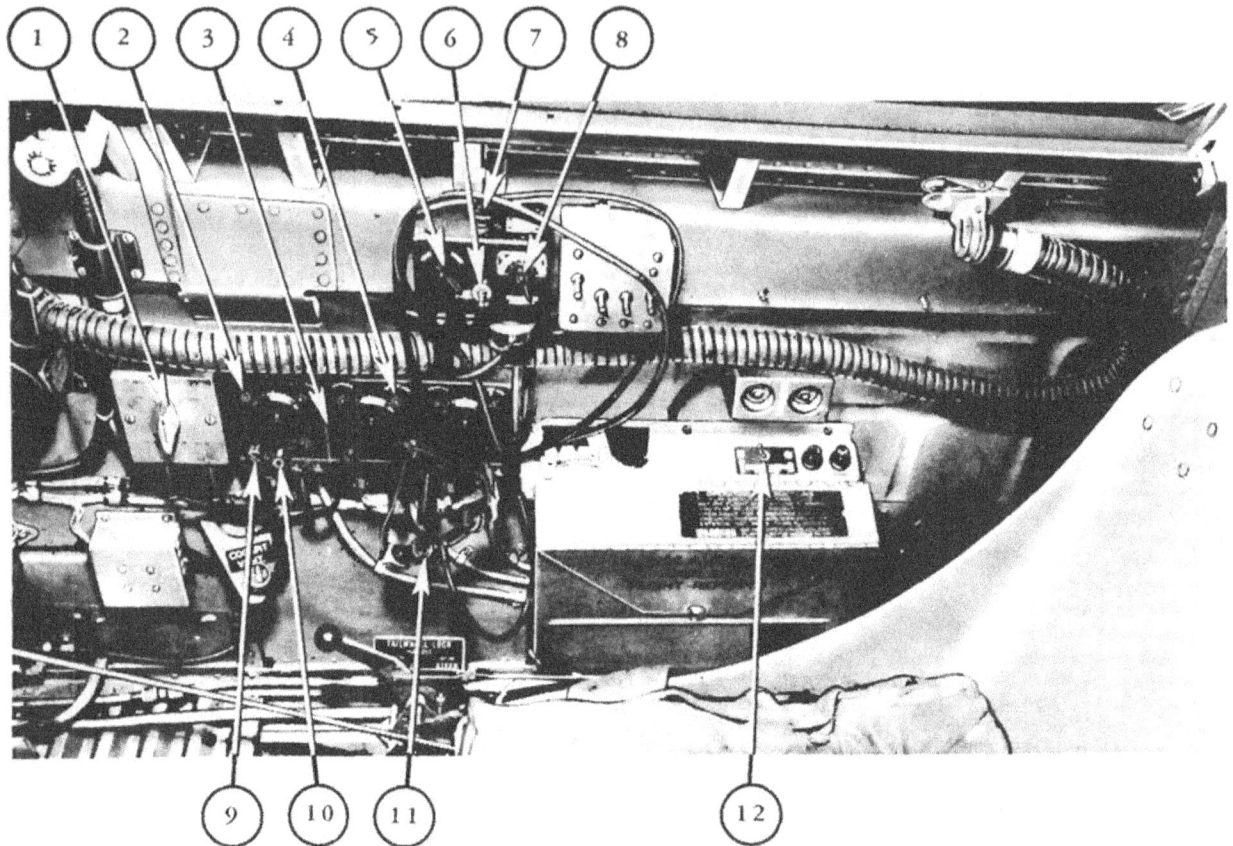

Figure 37—Radio Controls, P-47C, P-47D, and P-47G

the particular receiver to which it is electrically and mechanically connected. Reception of a signal of a specific frequency as indicated on the dial is accomplished by the use of the section of the receiver control box which controls the particular receiver involved.

(b) Plug head set phone jack plug in jack. Turn volume control (figure 37-9) to right until a faint frying noise is heard in the head set.

(c) Set crystal filter selector switch (figure 37-1) on "BOTH" for all normal (voice or MCW) reception.

(d) Turn switch (figure 37-4) on. This switch, in addition to having an "OFF" position, has two selective positions marked "CW" and "MCW," each of which is an "ON" position and indicates the type of signal which is to be received.

NOTE

When tuning receiver for a definite frequency, always turn dial a little to each side of the frequency calibration mark to find the point where the signal is the strongest.

(e) The "A-B" switches should be left in the "A" position at all times.

(3) TRANSMITTING.

(a) Before transmitting, adjust radio receiver to the same frequency as the station with which you desire to talk and listen in to be sure that the operator is not talking to someone else. If the station is transmitting, take advantage of the opportunity to more accurately set the receiver on the assigned frequency, and when the other operator is finished, proceed with your transmission.

(b) Place transmitter master switch (figure 37-6) in "ON" position.

(c) Select type of transmission desired with switch marked "TONE-CW-VOICE." (See figure 37-5.)

1. With switch in "VOICE" position, voice will be transmitted when the push-to-talk button (figure 35-9) is pressed.

2. With the switch in the "CW" position, a continuous wave, or unmodulated signal, will be transmitted. The microphone is inoperative.

3. With the switch in the "TONE" position, a modulated tone signal is transmitted. The microphone is inoperative.

NOTE

Greatest effective range can be obtained on "CW." Range is most limited when operating on "VOICE." Transmitting in both the "CW" and "VOICE" positions is done by a key (figure 37-7) located on the top of the transmitter control unit.

4. To reduce battery drain and to increase dynamotor life, the "TONE-CW-VOICE" switch (figure 37-5) should be left on "VOICE" unless continued use on "CW" or "TONE" is expected.

c. RADIO SET SCR-522-A (UHF).

(1) GENERAL.

(a) This equipment is an ultra high frequency (UHF) command set designed for voice communication only. It is used in conjunction with a contactor (pip squeak) for identification and navigational purposes.

(b) The radio waves from this equipment travel in straight lines, like beams of light, and do not follow the curvature of the earth. Due to this fact, in order to receive signals from a ground station, it is necessary that the airplane be above a certain altitude, the altitude being determined by the distance of the airplane from the ground station.

1. If the airplane is between 35 and 50 miles away from the ground station, it must be above 1000 feet before reception is possible.

2. If the airplane is between 80 and 100 miles away from the ground station, it must be above 5000 feet before reception is possible.

3. If the airplane is between 120 and 160 miles away from the station, it must be above 10,000 feet before reception is possible.

NOTE

If the range differs from any of the above-mentioned distances, altitude will change proportionately.

(c) Excessive operation of this equipment on the ground must be avoided unless a battery cart is used to prevent running down the airplane's battery.

(2) OPERATION.

(a) Press the proper channel button on the cockpit control box for the frequency upon which you are to transmit and receive.

NOTE

Transmission and reception take place on the same frequency.

(b) The green pilot light (figure 38-4) adjacent to the channel button, pressed, lights up whenever the set is in operation.

(c) The white pilot light adjacent to the toggle switch (figure 38-5) should light up, indicating that the set is on "RECEIVE."

(d) For throttle microphone button transmission, the toggle switch (figure 38-6) must be in the "REM" position.

NOTE

"REM"(Remote) was marked "V.O." on early control boxes.

(e) Press microphone button, press the throttle microphone "push-to-talk" button, and speak in a loud voice with the microphone against your lips. The white pilot light goes out, indicating that the set is on "transmit."

(f) It is also possible to transmit by moving the control box toggle switch (figure 38-6) to the "T" position, instead of pressing the throttle push-to-talk button. However, it must be returned to either the "R" or "REM" position immediately after transmission is completed in order to receive.

(g) Indicator lamps on the control box are provided with a dimmer mask for night flying. The mask is operated by moving a small lever beside the "OFF" pushbutton (figure 38-3).

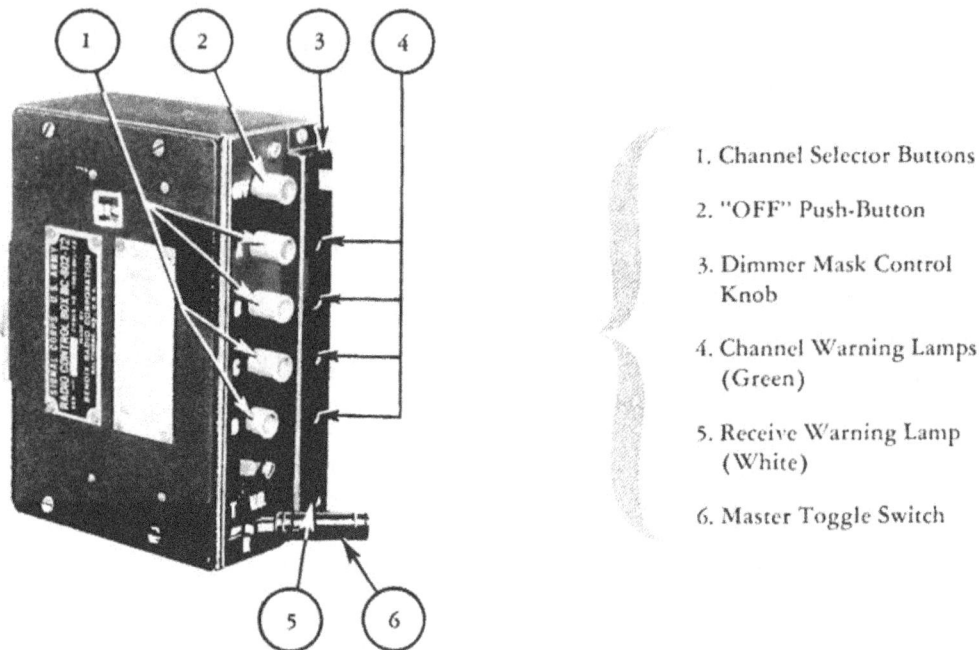

1. Channel Selector Buttons

2. "OFF" Push-Button

3. Dimmer Mask Control Knob

4. Channel Warning Lamps (Green)

5. Receive Warning Lamp (White)

6. Master Toggle Switch

Figure 38—Control Box—Radio Set SCR-522

d. CONTACTOR RC-96 (PIP SQUEAK).

(1) The contactor is used with either the SCR-274N or SCR-522A command sets.

(2) When the contactor clock on the instrument panel (figure 31-22) is turned on, the transmitter is in operation. It sends out a 14-second tone signal once every minute on channel "D" when used with the SCR-522 radio set and on channel 2 when used with the SCR-274N set. Transmission of the signal occurs during the period that the hand is moving through the marked quadrant on the face of the clock.

(3) Connect contactor clock to radio set by placing switch (figure 31-21) in the "IN" position.

(4) Start clock by placing clock master switch (figure 31-23) in the "RUN" position.

(5) When the clock takes over, the channel selector switch automatically goes to the proper channel and a continuous tone is heard both in the phones and on the ground for 14 seconds. At the end of the 14-second signal period, the selector switch automatically switches back to the original channel.

WARNING

It is impossible to transmit or receive voice during the 14-second tone signal period.

e. RADIO SET SCR-535 (IFF).

(1) The control box for this radio set is located on the right side of the cockpit. A master switch is located on the box. Operation of the set is automatic and the pilot has only to place the switch in the "ON" position to place the equipment in operation.

(2) A dual push-button switch, painted red, is located on the right side of the cockpit above the map case (figure 33-7). The purpose of the two push buttons is to destroy the IFF equipment should it be necessary to abandon the airplane over unfriendly territory. When both push buttons are pressed simultaneously, a detonator is set off in the receiver which is located in the aft end of the fuselage in the baggage compartment. The explosion of the detonator will destroy the receiver internally. No damage to the airplane will result at the time of destruction of the set.

NOTE

Regeneration adjustment of the IFF set must be made on the ground prior to flight in order to insure correct operation of the equipment.

SECTION V

ARMAMENT

1. GUN SIGHT OPERATION.

The airplane is equipped with an N-3A sight. The brilliance of the sight reticle is adjustable by means of a rheostat (figure 18-12) on the main switch panel on the left side of the cockpit below the throttle. The reticle is visible only when the eyes are in the proper position, within a 2-inch circle directly behind the sight. In some eye positions, only a portion of the outer ring is visible, but this in no way affects the accuracy of the sight.

2. GUNS.

Eight .50-caliber guns, four in each wing, are provided. Only six guns, with ammunition, are included in the design useful load. Two guns and ammunition are alternate load. No rounds indicators are provided. The maximum load is 425 rounds each. Desired loading with six guns is 300 rounds each and with eight guns, 200 rounds each. These guns are charged manually on the ground before take-off. Determine the loading for each particular flight in order to estimate the firing time. Three hundred (300) rounds of ammunition is approximately twenty seconds of fire.

3. GUN OPERATION.

Since the guns have been previously loaded and charged on the ground, they are ready to fire immediately when the safety switch installed on the left wheel of the cockpit is turned "ON." The squeeze trigger on the stick fires all guns simultaneously. If one or more guns should jam, the others will continue to operate effectively. THE GUN SAFETY SWITCH SHOULD BE IN THE "OFF" POSITION BEFORE LANDING.

4. BORE-SIGHTING.

The guns may be bore-sighted in a horizontal plane from a position where each gun is parallel to the other, to a position where all guns converge at 250 yards, and in a vertical plane from intersection with the sightline at 250 yards and 85% maximum speed at best performing altitude to intersection at 250 yards at full speed at best performing altitude. Ordinarily the guns are set to converge at 250 yards or 350 yards. Figure 41 shows the ranges for each setting through which effective firing may be accomplished. Determine the bore-sighting position of your guns before take-off on a firing mission.

Figure 39—Gun Heat Control

Figure 40—Gun Safety Switch

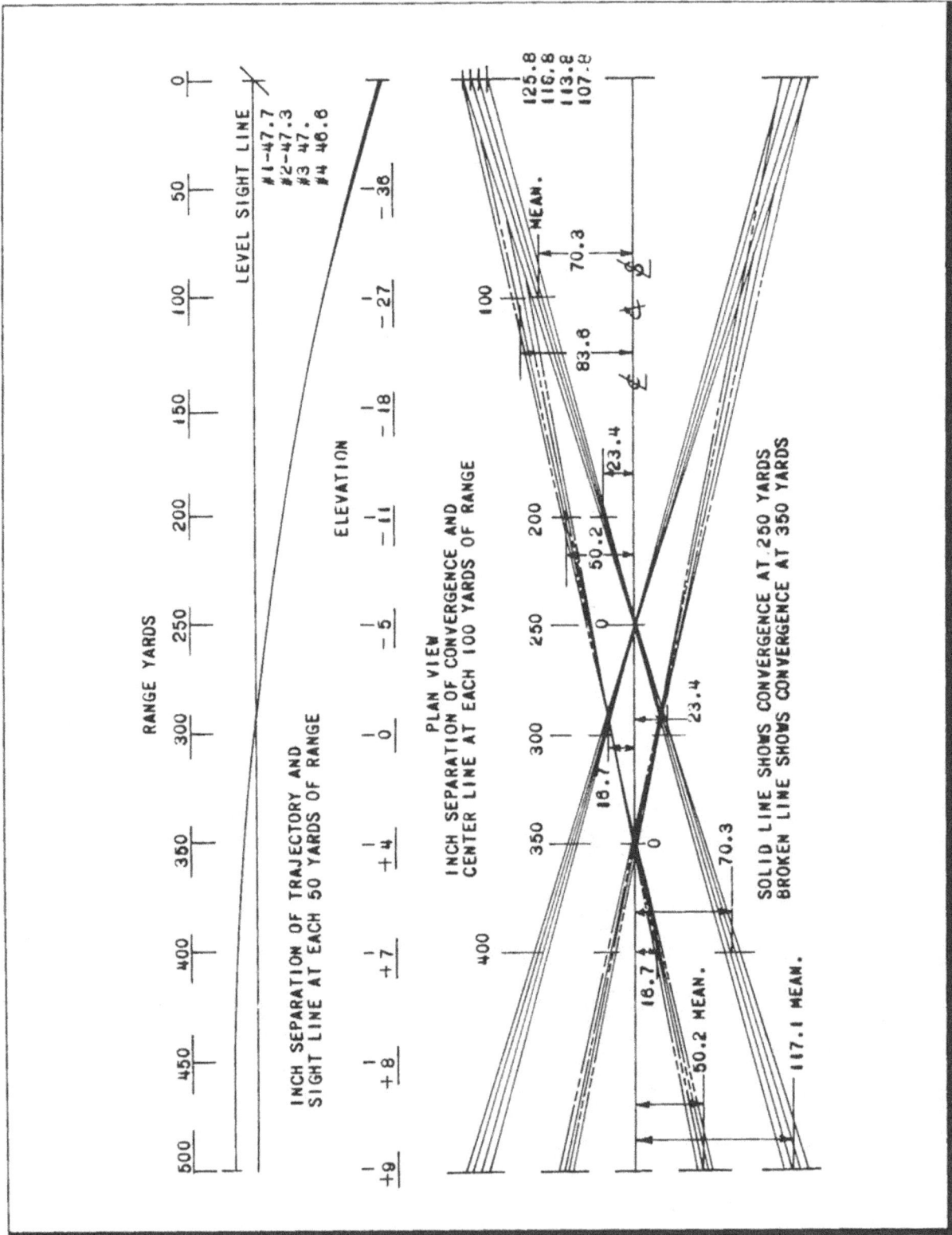

Figure 41—Gun Elevation and Convergence Diagram—P-47B, P-47C and P-47G

SECTION VI
OPERATION OF OXYGEN EQUIPMENT

1. DEMAND TYPE SYSTEM.

a. PREFLIGHT CHECK.

(1) GENERAL.—Before using this equipment, be sure you are familiar with the complete oxygen demand system. Consult your Oxygen Officer and refer to the applicable Technical Orders, the Lithograph Instruction Charts, and Trailing Films on oxygen equipment. Thoroughly understand the operation, use, and purpose of each instrument and item. Give each part the care and consideration it requires for its proper functioning.

(2) MASK.

(a) The mask must be properly fitted and checked for leakage by the Oxygen Officer. Flights over 30,000 feet must not be made when the mask leak is greater than 5%.

(b) Check all parts of the mask to see if it is in good shape and ready for instant use. The mask must be clean and free of all foreign matter.

Figure 42—Engine Primer Cowl Flaps
and Oxygen Controls

(c) Try the mask on in the airplane and check for leaks by holding the thumb over the corrugated hose fitting and inhaling normally.

(3) QUICK DISCONNECT FITTING. — Insert the male fitting (see that the gasket is in place) of the mask into the female end of the tubing from the regulator. Be sure the fit is snug and that a pull of at least 10 pounds is required to separate the two.

(4) MASK-REGULATOR TUBING.

(a) Inspect the mask-regulator tubing for any damages, such as tears, holes, and kinks. Be sure all clamps are firmly in place.

(b) Attach the tubing, by means of the spring clip on the female fitting, to the clothing or parachute harness high up on the chest. It may be desirable to sew on a tab of fabric or webbing to the clothing to accommodate the clip. Be sure that the attachment is high enough so that there is free movement of the head without kinking the mask hose. Be sure that the mask hose does not become kinked or twisted in flight.

(5) REGULATOR AND INDICATING INSTRUMENTS.

(a) Be sure that the knurled collar at the outlet end of the regulator is tight. Examine the top diagram to see that it is not ruptured or distorted.

(b) Turn on the "EMERGENCY" valve and see that you get a large flow. Observe the pressure gage. There should be no perceptible pressure drop. Turn "OFF" the "EMERGENCY" valve tightly, and be sure that it does not leak. Leave it in this position.

(c) Turn the "AUTO-MIX" to the "OFF" position. Notice that on inhalation the top diaphragm goes down and that you gear nearly 100% oxygen, which will be indicated on the flow indicator. Turn the "AUTO-MIX" to the "ON" position. Notice that on inhalation you get almost pure air and that there is little or no indication of oxygen flow on the flow indicator. Leave it in this position.

(d) Check the pressure of the system. It must not be less than 400 pounds per square inch.

b. IN FLIGHT.

(1) Manipulate the mask to free it of ice at regular intervals when temperatures are low enough to cause ice formation in the mask.

RESTRICTED

(2) Be sure that your mask hose does not become kinked or twisted.

(3) Be sure that your mask does not lose its leak-proof characteristics.

(4) If for any reason you feel you are suffering from lack of oxygen, if your mask should suddenly leak, if the demand mechanism fails, or if no oxygen flow is indicated by the flow indicator, immediately turn on the "EMERGENCY" control on the regulator.

(5) Check the oxygen pressure gage frequently.

(6) Check the flow indicator frequently.

(7) In any flight over 30,000 feet, pay particular attention to your oxygen equipment. Be sure all items and instruments are functioning perfectly before attempting flight to these extreme altitudes. Any failure of the equipment may be fatal.

c. AFTER FLIGHT.

(1) Be sure that all oxygen equipment is in proper condition before leaving the airplane. If any difficulties developed during the flight, take necessary steps to have them corrected.

(2) If your pressure is less than 100 pounds per square inch, observe that the supply warning light is on. Occasionally, at the end of a flight, when the pressure is slightly above 100 pounds per square inch, bleed the oxygen out of the system by opening the "EMERGENCY" on the regulator and see that the supply warning light goes on at about 100 pounds per square inch. Then turn the "EMERGENCY" off.

(3) Wash the mask with mild soap and water, dry thoroughly, and leave in a clean, airy place out of the sunlight.

(4) At all times, be sure that the mask is in good condition and is properly fitted for instant use.

2. CONSTANT FLOW TYPE.

a. PREFLIGHT CHECK.

(1) GENERAL.—Before using this equipment, be sure you are familiar with the complete oxygen system. Consult your Oxygen Officer and refer to the applicable Technical Orders, the Lithograph Instruction Charts, and Training Films on oxygen equipment. Thoroughly understand the operation, use, and purpose of each instrument and item. Give each part the care and consideration it requires for its proper functioning.

(2) MASK.

(a) The mask must be properly fitted. Check all parts of the mask to see if it is in good shape and

Figure 43—Oxygen Flow Regulator
P-47C, P-47D and P-47G

ready for instant use. Particular attention should be paid to the condition of the bag. The mask must be clean and free of all foreign matter.

(b) Be sure that the component parts of the mask are securely held together with wire or tape. Be sure that the plug at the bottom of the bag and the sponge rubber valves are in proper position.

(c) If flight is to be made under freezing conditions, have the plastic connector between the face-piece and the bag sticking up inside the facepiece above the lower surface, so that moisture will not readily drain into the connector and bag. Protective shields, drawing No. 43B8375, should be used for the sponge rubber valves.

(d) Be sure that the bayonet fitting at the end of the mask hose has its rubber gasket and that proper connection can be made with the outlet fitting on the regulator.

(3) REGULATOR.

(a) Check the cylinder or system pressure as shown on the regulator gage. It must be at least 400 pounds per square inch.

(b) Turn the needle valve knob on and see that there is no restriction to flow. This adjustment knob should not be too loose. If it is, tighten the gland packing which is on the same shaft.

(c) Check the regulator for proper flow with the ground flow check meter, Specification No. 40400.

b. IN FLIGHT.

(1) Be sure to set the regulator to the proper altitude.

(2) Manipulate the mask to free it of ice at regular intervals when temperature is low enough to cause ice formation in the mask.

(3) Be sure that your mask hose does not become kinked or twisted.

(4) Be sure that your mask retains its proper fit.

(5) Check the oxygen gage on the regulator frequently.

(6) Above 30,000 feet the bag should never be completely collapsed during inhalation. If it is, the adjustment knob on the regulator should be opened farther, no matter what the flow indicator setting is.

(7) When activity is required, the flow should be also increased so that the bag does not completely collapse.

c. AFTER FLIGHT.

(1) Be sure that the regulator adjustment knob is tightly closed so that there is no leakage.

(2) Be sure all the oxygen equipment is in proper condition before leaving the airplane. If any difficulties developed during the flight, take necessary steps to have them corrected.

(3) Wash the mask with mild soap and water, dry thoroughly, and leave in a clean, airy place out of the sunlight.

(4) At all times, be sure that the mask is in good condition and is properly fitted for instant use.

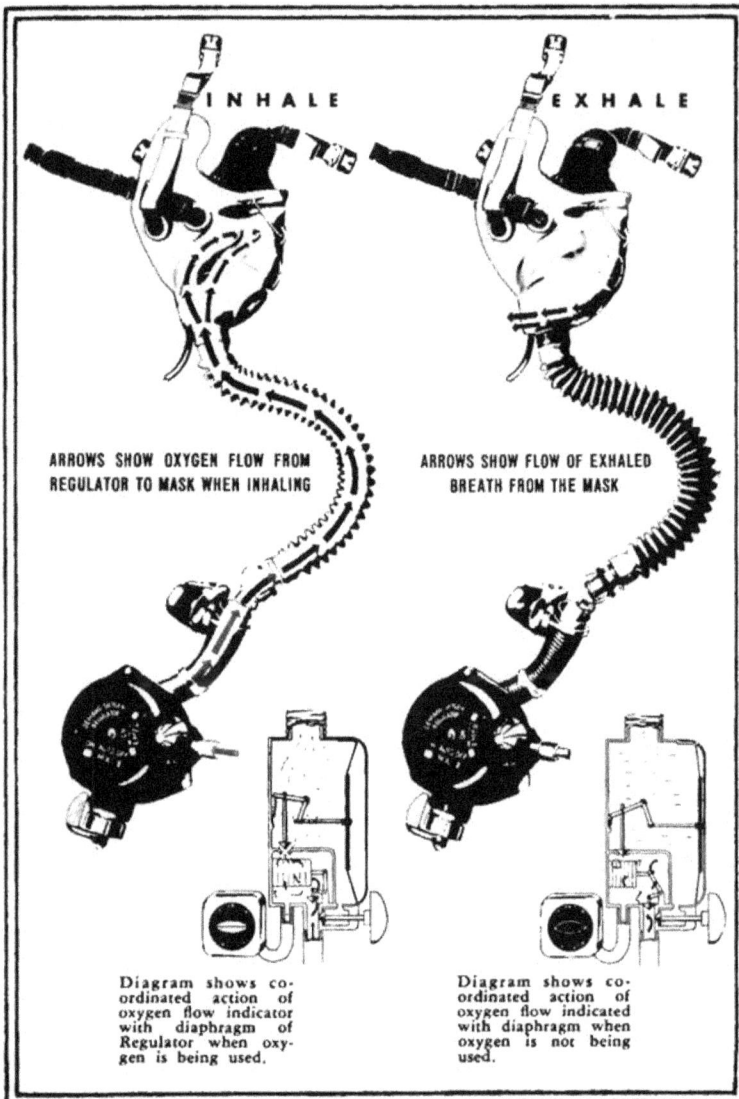

DIAGRAM OF OXYGEN MIXTURE AT 30,000 FEET

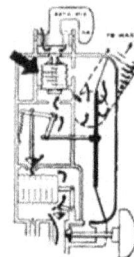

At 30,000 feet and above, the Auto-Mix sylphon because of barometric pressure shuts off all outside air, permitting only pure oxygen to flow through the Regulator. Green arrows indicate the movement of oxygen from the supply line to the mask.

DIAGRAM OF OXYGEN MIXTURE AT 10,000 FEET

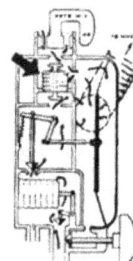

At intermediate altitudes the Auto-Mix sylphon controls a variable mixture of oxygen and air. The percentage of oxygen depending on the altitude. All of this is automatically controlled by the action of sylphon. The higher the altitude the greater is the percentage of oxygen flow. The black arrows indicate incoming air and the green arrows indicate the incoming oxygen.

DIAGRAM OF OXYGEN MIXTURE AT SEA LEVEL

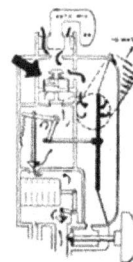

At sea level the Auto-Mix sylphon is completely depressed because of the barometric pressure; thus stopping most of the oxygen flow through the Regulator. Black arrows in illustration show the incoming air as it flows through the Auto-Mix into the Regulator and to the mask. Small green arrows indicate trickle of oxygen flow into mixing chamber.

INHALE — ARROWS SHOW OXYGEN FLOW FROM REGULATOR TO MASK WHEN INHALING

Diagram shows coordinated action of oxygen flow indicator with diaphragm of Regulator when oxygen is being used.

EXHALE — ARROWS SHOW FLOW OF EXHALED BREATH FROM THE MASK

Diagram shows coordinated action of oxygen flow indicated with diaphragm when oxygen is not being used.

FOR USE IN CASE OF EMERGENCY

Prior to flight always check this knurled collar. It must be TIGHT.

If Regulator fails to function, turn on Emergency Valve. This allows a constant flow of oxygen to the mask direct from the supply line. Flow indicator will not operate under this condition, and oxygen will flow from the supply line at a higher rate. Watch your pressure gage.

EMERGENCY "ON"

When Emergency Valve is opened the green arrows indicate the flow of oxygen from supply line direct through the Emergency Valve and Regulator to the mask.

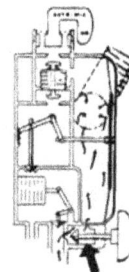

Figure 44—Oxygen Operating Instructions, P-47C, P-47D, and P-47G

Illustration shows the A-9 Oxygen Mask in position at left side of helmet ready for quick attachment on face. When not in use leave mask attached to helmet as shown.

Here the A-9 Mask is being attached with straps in uncrossed position on helmet. This method recommended for broad or full faces. Mask must not leak. To check this, hold thumb over end of mask hose. If leaks occur around face, adjust straps or nose wire to fit mask more securely and test again.

Illustration shows the A-10 Oxygen Mask being attached with straps in crossed position to the rear of the "Juliet." This cross position of straps is recommended for small, or long and narrow faces, as it makes a firm and leak-proof fitting.

For normal operation the "Auto-Mix" should always be turned to "ON" position as noted here. This assures a proper mixture of oxygen with the outside air.

Here the nose strap (distinguishing difference between the A-9 and the A-10 Masks) is being fixed to the front of the "Juliet" in regular supporter-like manner. This helps to hold the mask in position. Check for leaks, following the method suggested for testing the A-9 Oxygen Mask.

To get oxygen, place the end connection of mask hose into the fitting, on end of feeder hose coming from the Demand Regulator.

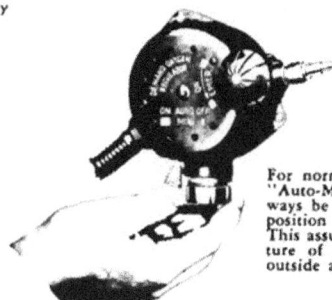

If regulator fails to function, turn on emergency valve illustrated above.

EMERGENCY GAS ABSORBING CANISTER

Gas canisters are furnished for all flying personnel to provide for protection against gas attacks while in flight or when landing on gassed terrain. Grasp canister near bottom and pull loose. This will automatically release both seals, making it ready for immediate use.

Before detaching oxygen mask hose from regulator connecting hose, take a deep breath. Then, before attaching the mask hose to the gas canister, exhale sufficiently to clear the mask and hose itself of any possible gas accumulation. Immediately thereafter, attach gas canister to mask hose, by inserting connection end into top of canister. Fasten canister to clothing by means of clip affixed to it.

To use the regulator chemical warfare service training canister, attach a small section of rubber tubing to it, replacing cork stopper to end of tube. This should be done before ascent. In attaching it to the oxygen mask, remove the corks, top and bottom, and thus proceed in the same manner as with the aircraft gas canister.

Figure 45—Oxygen Mask Instructions—P-47C, P-47D, and P-47G

APPENDIX I
U.S.A.-BRITISH GLOSSARY OF
NOMENCLATURE

Accumulator (hydraulic)	Should not be confused with electrical accumulator or battery
Airfield	Aerodrome
Battery (electrical)	Electrical accumulator
Bombardier, bomber	Bomb aimer
Ceiling	Cloud height
Empennage	Tail unit
Flight indicator	Artificial horizon
Gasoline (gas)	Petrol
Glass, bullet-proof	Armour glass
Gross weight	All up weight
Ground (electrical)	Earth
Gyro horizon	Artificial horizon
Gyro pilot	Automatic pilot
(to) Land	(to) Alight
Lean	Weak
Left	Port
(to) Level off	(to) Flatten out
Line, mooring	Mooring guy
Manifold pressure	Boost
Mast, radio	Rod aerial
Overload	Non-standard load
Panel, outboard	Outer plane
Reticle (gun sight)	Graticule
Screen	Filter
Set, command	Pilot controller set
Ship	Aircraft
Speed, indicated air (IAS)	Air-speed-indicator reading
Stabilizer, horizontal	Tail plane
Stabilizer, vertical	Fin
Stack	Manifold (inlet or exhaust)
Tachometer	Engine speed indicator
Tube (radio)	Valve
Turn indicator	Direction indicator
Valve (fuel or oil)	Cock
Weight empty	Tare
Windshield	Windscreen
Wing	Main plane

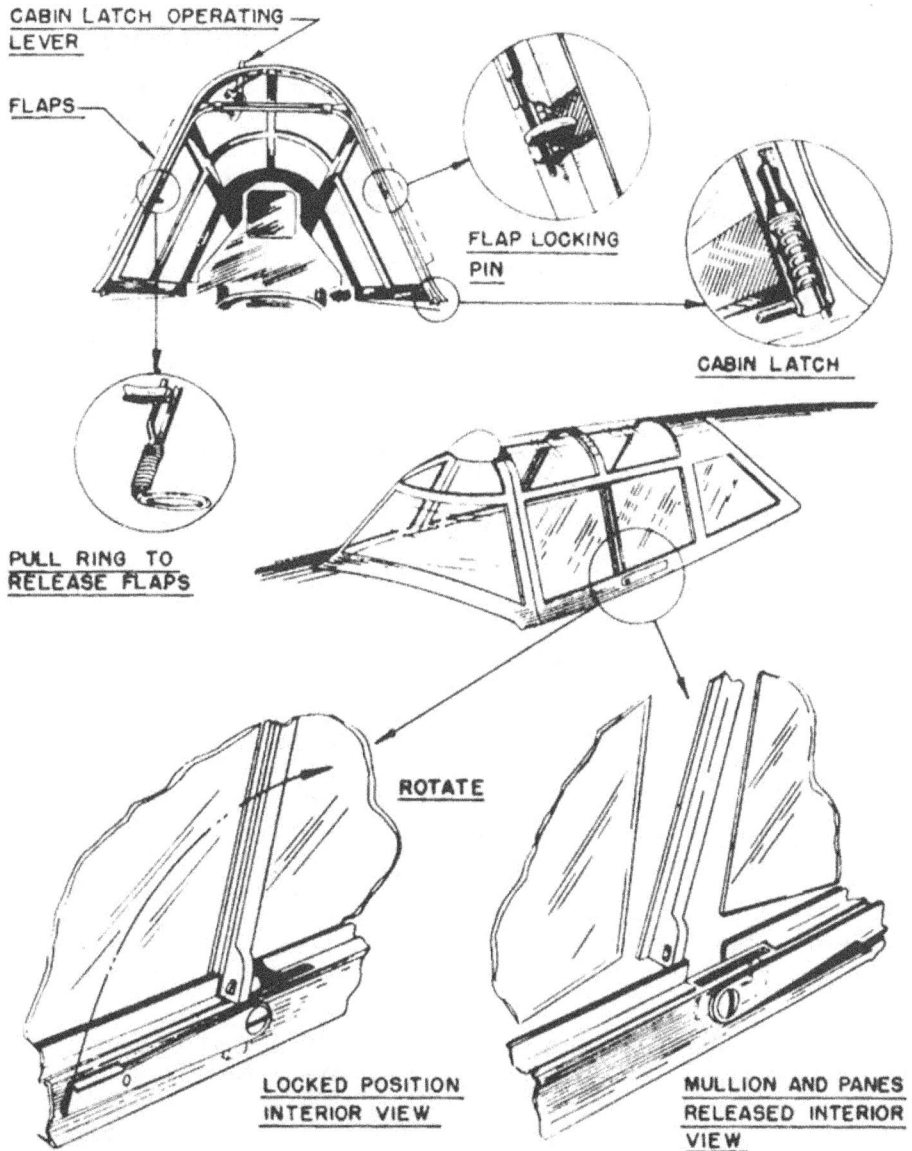

CABIN LATCH OPERATING LEVER

FLAPS

FLAP LOCKING PIN

CABIN LATCH

PULL RING TO RELEASE FLAPS

ROTATE

LOCKED POSITION INTERIOR VIEW

MULLION AND PANES RELEASED INTERIOR VIEW

FOR EMERGENCY EXIT, ROTATE LEVER UP AND AFT 180° THIS RELEASES THE MULLION BETWEEN THE TWO SIDE PANES WHICH THEN MAY BE PUSHED OUT.

FIG. 46 CANOPY-EMERGENCY EXIT

Figure 46—Canopy—Emergency Exits Diagram

APPENDIX II

EMERGENCY OPERATING
INSTRUCTIONS

1. EMERGENCY TAKE-OFF.

Use oil dilution to obtain proper oil pressure at moderate power, and as soon as the engine will take the throttle, taxi out, and *take off*.

WARNING

Apply throttle slowly but steadily. Sudden application of full throttle greatly affects torque.

2. ENGINE FAILURE DURING TAKE-OFF.

a. Nose down.

b. Land on field STRAIGHT AHEAD. If too late, retract gear and land OFF FIELD STRAIGHT AHEAD.

CAUTION

DO NOT ATTEMPT TO TURN BACK INTO THE FIELD.

3. ENGINE FAILURE DURING FLIGHT.

a. Nose down.

b. Ignition switch "OFF." (To "BAT" on P-47 only.)

c. If airplane is equipped with a belly tank, pull release lever immediately.

d. Fuel selector valve "OFF."

e. Manually lower the flaps.

f. Master battery switch "OFF" (P-47C, -D, and -G only).

g. If a suitable emergency airfield is available, the landing gear may be lowered. If not, keep landing gear "UP" and LAND AIRPLANE ON ITS BELLY.

4. EMERGENCY EXIT DURING FLIGHT.

a. Release canopy lock and push canopy back in the usual manner. At high speeds, pull the handle on the right forward edge of the canopy, releasing spoiler flaps which aid in sliding canopy back.

b. To release panels, turn the emergency release handle 180 degrees until it snaps into place. Push out the partition between the windows. Push out windows.

5. EMERGENCY ENTRANCE ON GROUND.

Remove the red cover plate at the lower edge of the canopy, on either side and pull out the handle thus exposed. Pull out the partition between the two panes by means of the ring located at its lower end. Pull out the panes.

6. WING FLAP OPERATION.

In event of failure of the engine-driven hydraulic pump, the flaps may be manually lowered by use of the emergency hand pump located at the left of the pilot's seat.

7. LANDING GEAR OPERATION.

a. FAILURE OF ENGINE-DRIVEN HYDRAULIC PUMP.

(1) TO RETRACT LANDING GEAR.—Move control lever to "UP" position as usual. Operate the hand pump until the position indicator shows that the gear is "UP" and locked.

(2) TO EXTEND LANDING GEAR. — Move control lever to the "DOWN" position as usual. This will release the gear which should drop into position and lock due to its own weight. If it does not fully attain the locked "DOWN" position, operate the hand pump until the "locked" signal is given. If the gear is still not locked down, yaw the airplane from side to side.

WARNING

Always complete landing gear cycle if possible. If handle is moved to "UP," allow gear to go completely up, before changing valve. If handle is moved to "DOWN," allow gear to go completely down before changing control.

b. FAILURE OF ENTIRE HYDRAULIC SYSTEM. —Extend the landing gear by moving the control into the "DOWN" position as usual. This motion releases the gear which drops, due to its own weight, and usually falls to the fully extended and locked "DOWN" position. In case air pressure prevents one wheel from fully attaining the locked position, it can be shaken into place by yawing the airplane from side to side.

WARSHIPS DVD SERIES

WARSHIPS: CARRIER MISHAPS

AIRCRAFT CARRIER
MISHAPS
SAFETY AND TRAINING FILMS

-PERISCOPEFILM.COM-

DVD

NOW AVAILABLE ON DVD!

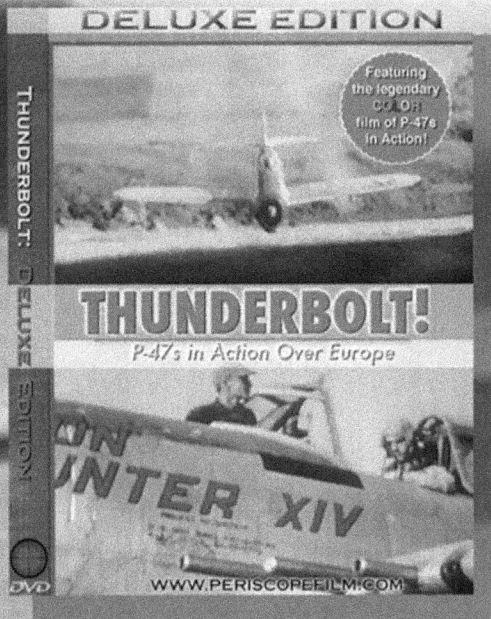

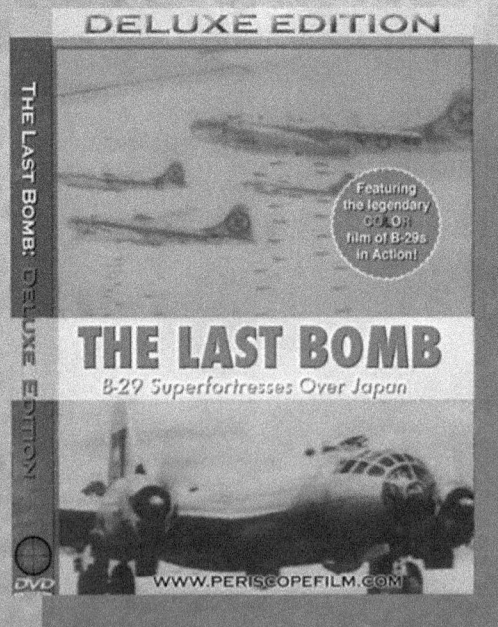

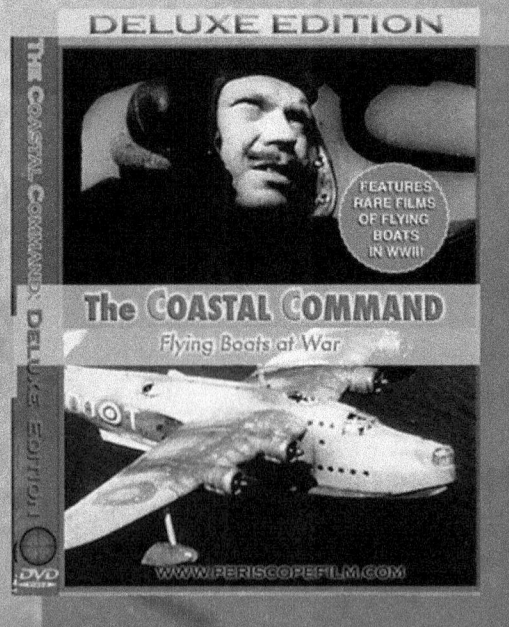

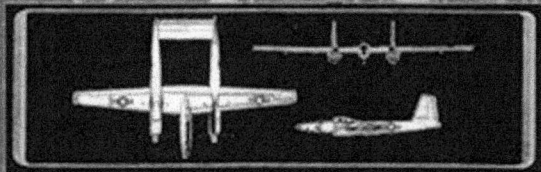

Originally Published by the U.S. Army Air Force
Reprinted by Periscope Film LLC

NOW AVAILABLE!

SPRUCE GOOSE

HUGHES FLYING BOAT MANUAL

~~RESTRICTED~~

Originally Published by the War Department
Reprinted by Periscope Film LLC

NOW AVAILABLE!

VOUGHT F4U-4 CORSAIR
PILOT'S FLIGHT OPERATING
INSTRUCTIONS

F4U-4 CORSAIR

NAVY 306

RESTRICTED

Originally Published by the U.S. Navy
Reprinted by Periscopefilm.com

THE FLEET TYPE
SUBMARINE

The definitive technical guide –
profiling the submarines
of World War II

RESTRICTED

Originally published as NAVPERS 16160
June 1946

WWW.PERISCOPEFILM.COM

CURTISS P-40 WARHAWK
PILOT'S FLIGHT OPERATING
MANUAL

FLYING TIGERS

RESTRICTED

Originally Published by the U.S. Army Air Force
Reprinted by Periscopefilm.com

NORTH AMERICAN X-15 ROCKET PLANE
PILOT'S FLIGHT OPERATING
INSTRUCTIONS

X-15 ROCKET PLANE

X-15

RESTRICTED

Originally Published by North American Aviation and the USAF
Reprinted by Periscopefilm.com

NORTHROP P-61 BLACK WIDOW
PILOT'S FLIGHT OPERATING
INSTRUCTIONS

NIGHT FIGHTER

RESTRICTED

Originally Published by USAAF July 1945
Reprinted by Periscopefilm.com

NORTHROP YB-49 FLYING WING
PILOT'S FLIGHT OPERATING
INSTRUCTIONS

FLYING WING

RESTRICTED

Reprinted by Periscopefilm.com

NORTH AMERICAN P-51 MUSTANG
PILOT'S FLIGHT OPERATING
INSTRUCTIONS

P-51 MUSTANG

RESTRICTED

B-17F
AIRPLANE

PILOT'S FLIGHT OPERATING
INSTRUCTIONS

B-17 F
AIRPLANE

Originally published by the
United States Army Air Forces
December, 1942.

RESTRICTED

LOCKHEED SR-71 BLACKBIRD
PILOT'S FLIGHT OPERATING
INSTRUCTIONS

SR-71 BLACKBIRD

RESTRICTED

Originally Published by Lockheed and the USAF

ALSO NOW AVAILABLE

FROM PERISCOPEFILM.COM

©2007-2010 Periscope Film LLC
All Rights Reserved
ISBN #978-1-935327-95-0   1-935327-95-X
www.PeriscopeFilm.com

www.ingramcontent.com/pod-product-compliance
Lightning Source LLC
Chambersburg PA
CBHW062108090426
42741CB00015B/3363